Dear Müller-Hartmann:

LETTERS FROM RALPH VAUGHAN WILLIAMS TO ROBERT MÜLLER-HARTMANN

STEVEN K. WHITE

ISBN 978-0-578-03584-0

"To Eva"

"But in the next world, I shan't be doing music, with all the strivings and disappointments... I shall be being it."

RALPH VAUGHAN WILLIAMS

Acknowledgements

I sincerely acknowledge the Vaughan Williams Charitable Trust, copyright holder of all Vaughan Williams's letters, for kindly granting permission to reproduce them. A number of people have helped tremendously during the compilation of this book. I especially thank Mr. Hugh Cobbe, former Head of Music Collections at the British Library, who was asked many years ago by Ursula Vaughan Williams to be the Archivist of Ralph Vaughan Williams's letters. Now the Director of the Vaughan Williams Charitable Trust, Hugh generously supplied texts and notes for the portion of the letters that are in his database, helping enormously with my attempts to decipher Vaughan Williams's handwriting. Dr. Nicolas Bell, Curator of Music Manuscripts at the British Library, gave me unexpected amounts of kindness, time, information and enthusiasm. I am grateful to the Holst Foundation for granting permission to reproduce the letter Imogen Holst wrote to Robert Müller-Hartmann shortly after his arrival in England. I acknowledge the courtesy of the Manx National Heritage Library for granting permission to reproduce the image of the Mooragh Internment Camp on the Isle of Man and I particularly thank Ms. Wendy Thirkettle, Archivist of the Library, for her help. I also owe a debt of thanks to the kind staff at the Dorking Cemetery.

I thank my parents for many things, of course, but especially for fostering an appreciation of music that brings me so much pleasure. I express immense gratitude to Neal Smith for his technical assistance and constant support. I recognize the memories of my late friends Robert D. Smith and Nancy M. Sargis, both of whom in their own way encouraged my interest in the music of Ralph Vaughan Williams. This book would not have been possible had not my friend Carol Bacon provided the means for a rather serendipitous connection with Eva Hornstein, the daughter of Vaughan Williams's close friends.

Although this project was in the planning stages for a long time, it was Eva Hornstein that provided the impetus for me to bring it to fruition. She generously provided many hours of her time, on the telephone and in-person, and access to her unique and amazing wealth of knowledge and insight. In November of 2008 I happened to be at the Royal Festival Hall in London for what turned out to be the last concert of Ralph Vaughan Williams's music ever conducted by the late Richard Hickox. After the performance, through an introduction by Eva, I was honored to shake the hand of Michael Kennedy and experience a moment of "connection by proxy" to Vaughan Williams himself. Eva also introduced me to Oliver Neighbour, Hugh Cobbe's predecessor as Head of Music Collections at the British Library, and I genuinely enjoyed our brief conversation about Robert Müller-Hartmann.

Eva arranged my contact with Karen Joelson, a niece of Lisbeth and Robert Müller-Hartmann, who was fortunate to spend part of the summer of 1950 living with them in Dorking. As far as I know, Karen is the only person on the face of the earth with first-hand memories of the Müller-Hartmanns. She was wonderfully generous in talking with me about her remembrances and impressions of those months and I cannot thank her enough for sharing several family photographs. Karen enabled me to learn tidbits about personalities that otherwise would be forever unavailable.

For me, this has been a fascinating journey with an underlying theme of "friendship". Eva openly shared some very personal stories with me and through her I have developed a great fondness for the people that I have written about. I hope that I might now claim Eva as one of *my* friends. This book is dedicated to her.

Table of Contents

Part One:

Robert Müller-Hartmann
With the kind permission of Karen Joelson

Introduction

The letters from Ralph Vaughan Williams to Robert Müller-Hartmann span the time period between their meeting in 1938 and Müller-Hartmann's death in 1950. My point of view is not that of a biographer or a musicologist. Instead, it is from that of a layman who has an inexplicably intense and long-time connection with the music and life of Ralph Vaughan Williams. Others who knew him well have written important and scholarly documentation of Vaughan Williams's life, music and communications, notably Ursula Vaughan Williams, Roy Douglas, Simona Pakenham and, of course, Michael Kennedy. Hugh Cobbe is undoubtedly one of the current generation's greatest authorities on Vaughan Williams and his recent book *Letters of Ralph Vaughan Williams* (Oxford University Press, 2008) is the work of a master.

Mrs. Müller-Hartmann provided copies of these letters to Ursula for her use in writing what is probably the definitive biography of Vaughan Williams. The texts of many of them are contained in the letter database maintained by Hugh Cobbe; several appear in his *Letters of Ralph Vaughan Williams* and in Ursula Vaughan Williams's *R.V.W.: A Biography of Ralph Vaughan Williams* (Oxford University Press, 1964). However, many of the letters in this book might be publicly seen for the first time. They expand upon the perceived importance of their friendship, allow a glimpse into the development of their professional relationship and provide additional insight into the mind (and dry sense of humor) of Vaughan Williams. In some ways seeing the actual images of letters in RVW's legendary scrawl makes the words seem more personal.

Fifty years after his death, Ralph Vaughan Williams is increasingly regarded as one of the most important composers of the twentieth century. Arguably, he is one of the most important English composers of all time. He knew and understood his *Englishness*, which he eloquently related in a series of lectures given at Bryn Mawr College in 1932, later to be published as *National Music*. He had a life-long passion for the music of Bach, yet in most ways Vaughan Williams deliberately rejected German musical influence; his musical essence was derived from everything in the great *English* musical tradition. His great friend and composer Gustav Holst shared his nationalism and was an important "sounding board" for Vaughan Williams's ideas and compositions. The death of Holst in 1934 was devastating to Vaughan Williams, leaving a major void in his life. It would be Imogen Holst, daughter of Gustav Holst, and his new friends Genia and Yanya Hornstein that would introduce him to composer Robert Müller-Hartmann. In many ways, Müller-Hartmann assumed the role that Gustav Holst had played earlier in Vaughan Williams's life. Müller-Hartmann was a Jewish *German* refugee from Nazi Germany. Like his friends Imogen Holst and Genia Hornstein, Vaughan Williams shared a hatred of Nazi oppression and worked tirelessly to help refugees find work and assimilate into English culture.

Early on in the Nazi years, Vaughan Williams had once expressed a fear that German composer refugees might have a negative influence on the *Englishness* of English music, but his fears were quickly overcome. As improbable as it might initially seem, the two possibly became friends in part *because* Müller-Hartmann was German. They shared a passion for Bach and later by translating many of RVW's vocal compositions into German Müller-Hartmann would be able to increase the appreciation for Vaughan Williams's music outside of England. Vaughan Williams *understood* the greatness and universal appeal of Bach's Mass in B minor, for example, and he *believed* in the greatness and universal appeal of his own works. Indeed, much of Vaughan Williams's music transcends nationalism and the limitations of language.

Müller-Hartmann was an important composer in his own right and the high degree of respect Vaughan Williams had for him is readily apparent from reading the letters. Yet, he remains vastly under-recognized. Hopefully, these letters will promote interest in Robert Müller-Hartmann's life and his music.

In early correspondence Vaughan Williams typically used a salutation of "Dear *Dr.* Müller-Hartmann", and after December 18, 1941, "Dear *Mr.* Müller-Hartmann" ("Forgive me for making you out an academic!"). Paralleling the evolution of their friendship, eventually Vaughan Williams expressed a desire to soften formalities. It is interesting to see the change on January 4, 1945, when Vaughan Williams wrote, "May we stop this 'mistering' and 'doctoring'." Thereafter his greeting would be simply "*Dear Müller-Hartmann*".

Müller-Hartmann: Before 1938

Robert Gerson Müller was born in Hamburg, Germany on October 11, 1884. His father's name was Josef Müller and his mother's maiden name was Jenny Hartmann; as an honor to her, later in his life he changed his legal name to "Müller-Hartmann". He was born into a musical family. His father was a clarinetist and pianist, and through his grandmother he was related to the composer and conductor Paul Dessau. He married Elisabeth (Lisbeth) Asch, also from a Hamburg family, and they had three children together: Susanne, Rudolf and Dietrich. There is a family story that Lisbeth's parents gave their daughter a rather elegant and elaborate wedding reception in order to "give her a good sendoff since she was marrying a 'poor musician'." The 1934 Hamburg directory listing for their residence was "Tonkünstler, GBorst, Wolterst 32".

In his early years, Müller-Hartmann studied music composition, theory and pianoforte at the Sternsches Konservatorium[1] in Berlin. He later taught music theory at the Krüss-Färber-Konservatorium with fields of special interest that included harmony, counterpoint, form, instrumentation and composition. In 1923 he became Assistant Professor in Music Theory at the University of Hamburg. He was a music critic for Hamburg newspapers, was employed as a musical expert by the North German Radio and was a member of the State Examination Board for private teachers of music.

Like other Jewish musicians, Müller-Hartmann's future and that of his family changed forever when the Nazis took control of Germany. Anti-Semitic laws and the banishment of "Jewish music" began in March of 1933, just six weeks after Hitler seized power, and he was forced to leave the University. In order to make a living, he began teaching music at the Jewish School for Girls in Hamburg. The Emergency Committee in Aid of Displaced Foreign Scholars was formed in New York City that same year by American academicians for the purpose of employing German Scholars in American institutions.

---

[1] Merged with other schools and currently a part of Berlin University of the Arts.

Records from the Emergency Committee, now housed in the Manuscripts and Archives Division of The New York Public Library and only recently available, show that Robert Müller-Hartmann was seeking assistance as early as 1934. The Emergency Committee placed advertisements in various academic publications and letters were written on his behalf to the University of Southern California and Brooklyn College. The Committee also attempted to help other Jewish composers, including Hans Gal, Robert Hernried, Robert Kanta, Ernst Hermann Meyer, Bruno Eisner and Karl Weigl. However, in spite of their help and the assistance of a similar organization in England, he was unable to find work outside of Germany.

Besides teaching music at the Jewish School for Girls, Müller-Hartmann was able to find a more creative outlet. The Jüdischer Kulturbund (Jewish Culture League) was an organization formed in 1933 and monitored by the Ministry of Propaganda and Public Enlightenment headed by Joseph Goebbels. While urging citizens to have nothing to do with "Jewish" music, the Nazis intent for the Kulturbund was to allow Jewish artists to continue to perform in Germany, but only for Jewish audiences. Originally formed in Berlin by Dr. Kurt Singer, branches quickly formed throughout Germany. Müller-Hartmann became the artistic advisor for the Kulturbund in Hamburg, while his friend Berthold Goldschmidt directed the orchestra in Berlin and Hans Wilhelm (William) Steinberg built the orchestra in Frankfurt. Although initially encouraged, conditions about performances soon became more restrictive and the Nazis eventually changed their minds entirely about the Kulturbund. Some musicians, like Müller-Hartmann, Steinberg and Goldschmidt, were able to get out of Germany but after *Kristallnacht* many others like Singer died in concentration camps.

Family Tree of Robert Müller-Hartmann

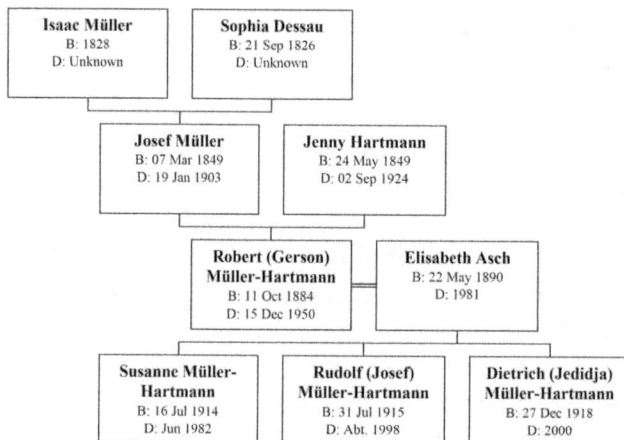

Isaac Müller
B: 1828
D: Unknown

Sophia Dessau
B: 21 Sep 1826
D: Unknown

Josef Müller
B: 07 Mar 1849
D: 19 Jan 1903

Jenny Hartmann
B: 24 May 1849
D: 02 Sep 1924

Robert (Gerson) Müller-Hartmann
B: 11 Oct 1884
D: 15 Dec 1950

Elisabeth Asch
B: 22 May 1890
D: 1981

Susanne Müller-Hartmann
B: 16 Jul 1914
D: Jun 1982

Rudolf (Josef) Müller-Hartmann
B: 31 Jul 1915
D: Abt. 1998

Dietrich (Jedidja) Müller-Hartmann
B: 27 Dec 1918
D: 2000

Elisabeth Müller-Hartmann
With the kind permission of Karen Joelson

Müller-Hartmann's Accomplishments

Robert Müller-Hartmann had impressive academic credentials for which Vaughan Williams must have had a great deal of respect. His teaching and journalistic abilities allowed him to work outside of the University while he was in Germany and with the help of Vaughan Williams and Imogen Holst, those same skills allowed him to gain employment in a foreign land. He found work as a music critic and writer for various newspapers, gave private music lessons and occasionally gave lectures for the BBC and other organizations.

In England he wrote a number of scholarly articles and letters: "Wieland's and Gluck's Versions of the 'Alkestis'", *Journal of the Warburg Institute*, Vol. 2, No. 2 (Oct., 1938); "Two Unknown Letters of Charles Burney", *Journal of the Warburg and Courtauld Institutes*, Vol. 3, No. 1/2 (Oct. 1939-Jan. 1940); "On Teaching Harmony", *Music and Letters*, Vol. XXVIII, No. 4 (1947); and "Reminiscences of Reger and Strauss", *Music and Letters*, Vol. XXIX, No. 2 (1948). Probably his most significant article, especially in the eyes of Vaughan Williams because of its relevance to Bach's Mass in B minor, was "A Musical Symbol of Death", *Journal of the Warburg and Courtauld Institutes*, Vol. 8 (1945).

However, the true spirit of Müller-Hartmann was that of a composer. In Germany his work was appreciated and held in high regard. A number of important conductors gave performances of his music, including Richard Strauss, Otto Klemperer, William Steinberg, Karl Muck, Hermann Abendroth and Fritz Busch. In England during the 1940s orchestras of the BBC performed some of his works.

He wrote a fairly large number of compositions, well over one hundred.[2] His "claim to fame", probably, was the *Overture to Georg Büchner's 'Leonce and Lena'*, which was premiered by Otto Klemperer in 1923 in Cologne. He wrote chamber music and original orchestral works, including a symphony. He made arrangements of music by Bach, Handel, Mozart,

---

[2] See *LexM* [Encyclopedia of Persecuted Musicians of the NS-Time] for a fairly complete listing of his compositions.

Telemann and Pachelbel. He composed songs with words in English as well as German. Much of his music was instrumental, notably for pianoforte, but he also wrote for organ, flute and strings. In England his music publishers included Novello and Co., J. Curwen and Sons and Hinrichsen Edition. Some of his piano arrangements, including G. F. Handel's *Arrival of the Queen of Sheba*, are still in print but unfortunately in current catalogs there are no available commercial recordings of his music.

Life in Dorking

Dorking is a place where the lives of the Vaughan Williamses, the Hornsteins and the Müller-Hartmanns would become intricately intertwined. In 1929 Adeline and Ralph Vaughan Williams moved there from 13 Cheyne Walk in Chelsea to a house on Westcott Road called "The White Gates", primarily because of Adeline's progressive rheumatoid arthritis and the need for more convenient living space.

The Hornsteins were refugees from the Russian Revolution. Eugenia (Genia) was born in St. Petersburg, Russia and moved with her family to Hamburg, Germany when she was thirteen years old. There, she married Jacob (Yanya) Hornstein who was born in Odessa, Ukraine. The Hornsteins were able to leave Germany and move to London around 1935 where Yanya found work. The Hornsteins and the Müller-Hartmanns must have known each other when they all lived in Hamburg; Susanne, the Müller-Hartmann's daughter, preceded the arrival of her parents and worked as a "nanny" for the Hornstein's daughters, Marianne and Renate.[3] In the late 1930s, to find the relative safety of a small town in Surrey, the Hornsteins moved to Dorking to a house on Ladyegate Road with the Welsh-derived name "Craigelly". Robert and Lisbeth Müller-Hartmann arrived in London in 1937, jobless and with little money. They first lived at 7 Durweston Mews, near Crawford Street, but within a short time they too made the move to Dorking and lived with the Hornsteins at Craigelly.[4] The Hornsteins and the Müller-Hartmanns shared, among other things, a common language, religion and experiences of disruption and persecution; they all had fled Nazi Germany.

Shortly after arriving in England, it is likely that Robert Müller-Hartmann became acquainted with Imogen Holst

---

[3] The Müller-Hartmann's two sons, Rudolf and Dietrich, left Germany in 1935 to help establish farming communities in Palestine (now Israel). They returned to Germany several times to help train others and eventually settled on a kibbutz.

[4] In later years Müller-Hartmann also kept an address in London, 68B Belsize Park Gardens (1939-1950s directories).

through her work helping German refugees at the Bloomsbury House in London; Ursula Wood volunteered there too.[5] Imogen Holst wrote to Müller-Hartmann on January 24, 1938, encouraging him to submit compositions to the BBC.[6] At her instigation, Vaughan Williams first wrote to Müller-Hartmann four days later.[7] To work in consort with the Bloomsbury House, the Dorking & District Refugee Committee was formed in December of 1938. Vaughan Williams first met Genia Hornstein during their work for the Dorking Committee and their shared sense of social activism was the foundation for a strong and lasting mutual friendship. For Vaughan Williams, personally and professionally, it was probably fortuitous that the Hornsteins and the Müller-Hartmanns had all decided to live beneath one roof. Vaughan Williams wrote to Müller-Hartmann, "I hear from Genia that you are coming to Craigelly – could we have some time together – I want to know more of your compositions – of which I know shamefully little (your fault, chiefly)."[8]

After the outbreak of war in September of 1939 the British government became very concerned with identifying "enemy aliens". Robert Müller-Hartmann had only just begun trying to build a new life in England, but by May of 1940 the political climate was such that a policy of mass internment of Jewish refugees was begun and Churchill ordered, "Collar the lot." In what must have been a horrendous and unimaginable time for his family and friends, he was forced to leave Dorking, sent by boat and interned in a camp on the Isle of Man with thousands of others.[9] The refugee committees, with great help from Vaughan Williams, were instrumental and successful in petitioning for the release of many musicians, academics and professionals. Vaughan Williams wrote to Müller-Hartmann:

[5] Adeline Vaughan Williams died on May 10, 1951. Ursula Wood and Ralph Vaughan Williams married on February 7, 1953.
[6] See Imogen Holst's letter (pp. 17-18).
[7] See Letter No. 01 (p. 26).
[8] See Letter No. 02 (p. 30).
[9] During WWII camps on the Isle of Man were located in the Douglas, Peel, Port Erin, Port Mary and Ramsey areas. See Manx National Heritage Library's *Internment During World Wars I & II*. The specific camp where Müller-Hartmann was interned has not been determined.

"May you soon be free to work for the country of your adoption and for the cause we all have at heart."[10] Müller-Hartmann was released from the camp on the Isle of Man in the autumn of 1940.

In the early years after Müller-Hartmann's release, Vaughan Williams wanted to help him gain financial independence and arranged various jobs for him, including music critic and copyist. As their friendship was developing, Müller-Hartmann wrote to Vaughan Williams thanking him for his kindness, telling him how fortunate he thought himself for living in Dorking and that learning about Vaughan Williams's music "helped me to change life in exile into an experience which I should not like to miss."[11] As the decade progressed, revealed by many of the letters Vaughan Williams wrote to Müller-Hartmann, his role became much more personal, collaborative and that of a respected colleague. In one very successful project, Müller-Hartmann translated Vaughan Williams's *Sancta Civitas* into German and he would later do the same with *The Pilgrim's Progress*.

*   *   *

In addition to her refugee work, Genia Hornstein was always active in many musical organizations. She was charismatic, vivacious and ebullient and spoke with a delightful Russian accent. She loved to entertain and in her later years, when visiting New York, she always *loved* to shop at Bloomingdale's.

Yanya Hornstein was quieter, more serious and perhaps comparatively a little "socially shy". For his company's business he frequently traveled to the United States and Europe. He enjoyed translating Russian poetry and transcribed a work by Nikolai Gumilev for one of Müller-Hartmann's *Ten English Songs*. Ursula once commented about his charming ability to use puns.

---

[10] See Letter No. 03 (p. 34).
[11] See *R.V.W.: A Biography of Ralph Vaughan Williams*, p. 252.

14

Lisbeth Müller-Hartmann was an intelligent and physically beautiful woman. Although in reality she was emotionally caring, she was somewhat reserved and perceived by most as "cool" – perhaps due to her personal situation. She spoke English well and also learned Hebrew so that she could write to her grandchildren in Israel. Typical of her generation, she was primarily a housewife and "took good care" of her husband and daughter.

Robert Müller-Hartmann was a kind, polite and truly "gentle" man. He had an excellent command of the English language, but like his wife, of course, he spoke with a heavy German accent. Having an innate ability to distinguish subtleties in musical tones, others sometimes found it humorous that he had difficulty choosing between words that sounded similar, e.g. "than" and "then", when conversing in English. He was very literate and read voraciously; Charles Dickens was his favorite author. A lover of opera, he also loved teaching people about opera while playing arias on the piano. Perhaps, in common with almost all other exiled Jewish musicians, he seemed somewhat "embittered" that circumstances prevented him from being perceived as more successful.

When her services as a "nanny" were no longer needed for the Hornsteins, Susanne Müller-Hartmann worked as a secretary for Yanya's company and enjoyed traveling overseas.

* * *

During the 1940s, Ralph and Adeline – and Ursula too – formed part of the social network with the Hornsteins and the Müller-Hartmanns. They spent time together after local concerts and many evenings were enjoyed at Craigelly. These were cultured, sophisticated "European" people; there were always intellectual conversations about current events, politics, literature, poetry and music. There were "musical" evenings at Craigelly too; sometimes Robert played the piano and sometimes Yanya played the cello. Frequently they critically listened to music on the phonograph – not just as background

15

music – but really "listened". When Vaughan Williams wasn't there, often they played recordings of his music. Along with others, the Müller-Hartmanns were regularly invited to The White Gates for live "play-through" performances of Ralph's new compositions.

Robert Müller-Hartmann became a British citizen in 1948. Vaughan Williams wrote "I feel it is a great honour to be able to claim you as a fellow citizen. I am glad to hear that you are doing a good deal of work for the BBC."[12] In early 1950, while Müller-Hartmann was working on the German translation of *The Pilgrim's Progress*, the three Müller-Hartmanns moved to their own home in Dorking on St. Paul's Road called "West Dene", a short walking distance from Craigelly. Only months after moving to West Dene, at a relatively young age, Robert Müller-Hartmann died suddenly from a cerebral hemorrhage on December 15, 1950. The funeral was in Dorking and his friend Yanya Hornstein gave the eulogy.[13] Vaughan Williams was extremely saddened and deeply affected by the death of his fellow composer and close friend, a relationship formed late in his life, and he would miss his ideas, his opinions and their regular talks. Undoubtedly his loss evoked emotions akin to those he felt in 1934 after the death of Gustav Holst.

---

[12] See Letter No. 39 (p. 136).

[13] After Robert Müller-Hartmann's death, Lisbeth and Susanne remained at West Dene for several years. Thereafter, they moved to London where they lived together at 19E Maresfield Gardens until Susanne became very ill with cancer. Toward the end of Susanne's illness, when she was no longer able to care for her mother, the elderly Mrs. Müller-Hartmann moved to Israel to live out the remainder of her days with her sons and grandchildren and died in 1981. Susanne died in June of 1982 at the age of sixty-eight.

from IMOGEN HOLST, 54 Ormonde Terrace, N.W.8   Primrose 4871

January 24th, 1938.

Dear Mr Müller-Hart,

I have not been able to get Miss Karpeles on the telephone, and tomorrow I have to be teaching in the country all day. But I will ring her up early on Wednesday morning, and will let you know immediately afterwards about our meeting at Cecil Sharp House on Thursday afternoon: — I am hoping that Douglas Kennedy, the Director of the English Folk Dance and Song Society, will be there as well, as I should like you to meet him.

Meanwhile, I am sending you my

Letter from Imogen Holst to Robert Müller-Hartmann, p. 1

17

note to Sir Adrian Boult, as I think you
should send your compositions to the B.B.C
at the first possible moment; — they will be
deciding on their programmes in a week or
ten days' time.

Yours sincerely,

Imogen Holst.

Letter from Imogen Holst to Robert Müller-Hartmann, p. 2

18

Mooragh Camp in Ramsey on the Isle of Man
© Manx National Heritage Library

Lisbeth at West Dene, 1950
With the kind permission of Karen Joelson

Rudolf (son), Lisbeth and Susanne Müller-Hartmann
With the kind permission of Karen Joelson

Epilogue

As it turns out, life in Dorking in the 1940s was much more interesting and modern than might be suspected. It seems there were complicated and perhaps compelling reasons why the Müller-Hartmanns had come to live with the Hornsteins at Craigelly: Yanya Hornstein was having an affair with his secretary Susanne, daughter of the Müller-Hartmanns, probably from the time she worked as the Hornstein's nanny; and Genia Hornstein was in love with Susanne's father, Robert Müller-Hartmann. Of course, as it is now generally known, Ursula and Ralph were in love too, at first while they were both still married to others. Ursula was probably one of the first to learn from Genia, even before the Hornstein's youngest daughter, Eva, was born that Robert Müller-Hartmann was actually her father. Although others in the circle also knew, except perhaps for Mrs. Müller-Hartmann, Eva did not learn for three and a half decades that her biological father was not the man she thought he was for all of those years, but instead the family friend she used to affectionately call "Harpo".

Robert Müller-Hartmann had died when she was just a young girl and her mother had died in 1970, so when she found out, Eva urgently went to Ursula with some questions. Apologetically, Ursula explained that the two best friends, after much discussion, had made a pact and "decided it was best" for Eva not to know the real story. While others might have felt hurt and deceived, Eva was genuinely *excited* and *enlightened*. Eva's adult life revolved around music and opera in particular. Although she never got the chance to really know him, when she learned that her father was actually an important composer and musician, all aspects of her life seemed to make sense and fall into place.

Craigelly Suite, undoubtedly, was written by Müller-Hartmann to express the great affection he had for the place and time. He used words written by Ursula Wood for two of the songs in *Ten English Songs*. It is hard to imagine that one of his last published works, *Eight Children's Songs*, was not composed, at least in part, with his young daughter, Eva, in

mind. Paying tribute to special friendships and relationships –
those that had their beginnings in the dark days of the Dorking
Refugee Committee – was also important to Vaughan Williams.
He dedicated *Partita for Double String Orchestra* to Robert
Müller-Hartmann, who played a major part in its re-working. *A
Winter Piece*, for pianoforte, was dedicated "For Genia, with
love from Uncle Ralph". Vaughan Williams acknowledged
Genia for her help making some final additions for the German
translation of his beloved opera, *The Pilgrim's Progress*, which
was left incomplete upon the death of Müller-Hartmann. "Uncle
Ralph" even made a fond attempt at writing a poem for then ten
year-old Eva, the daughter of his two great friends, when she
was ill:[14]

To Eva

> *I'm all in the dumps*
> *To think you have mumps.*
> *That's only for frumps*
> *(With protuberant humps*
> *Which stick out in lumps)*
> *That growls and that grumps;*
> *Not for EVA, who jumps*
> *In elegant pumps*
> *Surrounded by clumps*
> *Of lovers that bumps*
> *And stirs their young stumps*
> *To the sound of bright trumps*
> *While the drum loudly thumps.*

Eva remained a close, important and trusted friend of
Ursula Vaughan Williams. Some years later, after their
"conversation", Ursula and Eva made a day trip from London
down to Dorking and visited the beautiful Victorian-style
cemetery on Reigate Road on the eastern edge of town. They
stood for a while over the graves of Eva's parents, Genia and
Yanya. Then Ursula asked Eva, "Well, do you want to go see

---

[14] Also reproduced in *The Works of Ralph Vaughan Williams*, pp. 380-1.

your father?" What a surreal experience it must have been to walk just a few steps and look at Robert Müller-Hartmann's grave in the same cemetery. At the funeral service of Ralph Vaughan Williams on September 19, 1958, included in the group of closest friends – foremost among all of the world dignitaries and important people – were Eva, her oldest sister and her parents. After Ursula's death on October 23, 2007, Eva assumed a major role in helping to manage her affairs. On April 21, 2008, Eva was among those privileged few to stand again in Westminster Abbey, above the re-opened marble floor in the Musicians' Aisle, and actually view the exposed wooden casket containing the ashes of Ralph Vaughan Williams. It seems so fitting that the daughter of Robert Müller-Hartmann and Genia Hornstein, their cherished friends, witnessed the very moment Ralph and Ursula were brought back together.

Robert Müller-Hartmann's gravestone in Dorking, Surrey

Part Two:
The Letters

A number of these letters, where indicated, also appear in Hugh Cobbe's *Letters of Ralph Vaughan Williams* (Oxford University Press, 2008). Some of the letters that are contained in the RVW letter database maintained by Hugh Cobbe have been previously annotated.

As Hugh Cobbe explains in *Letters of Ralph Vaughan Williams*, Vaughan Williams rarely used the year when writing dates; therefore, many letters were somewhat difficult to place in chronological order. "Educated guesses" were used when more accurate dating was not possible. Vaughan Williams's handwriting, especially from his later years, is notoriously difficult to decipher; several words remain elusive.

No. 01
To Robert Müller-Hartmann[15]

From R. Vaughan Williams,
The White Gates,
Westcott Road,
Dorking.

January 27 [1938]

Dear Dr Müller-Hartmann

I venture to write to you at the instigation of our mutual friend Miss Imogen Holst.

I should very much like to make your acquaintance. Could you come to lunch with me at The Royal College of Music, Prince Consort Road near the Albert Hall at 1 o'clock next Wednesday February 2nd? It would give me great pleasure.

Yours sincerely

R. Vaughan Williams

---

[15] In the hand of Adeline Vaughan Williams, RVW's first wife, but signed by RVW. See also *R.V.W.: A Biography of Ralph Vaughan Williams*, p. 237.

01

FROM R. VAUGHAN WILLIAMS.

THE WHITE GATES,
WESTCOTT ROAD,
DORKING.

TELEPHONE
DORKING 1055

January 27,
1938

Dear Dr. Müller – Hartmann

I venture to write to you at
the instigation of our mutual
friend Miss Imogen Holst.

I should very much like to
make your acquaintance.
Could you come to lunch with
me at The Royal College of Music,
Prince Consort Road near the Albert
Hall at 1 o'clock next Wednesday

February 2nd? It would give
me great pleasure –

Yours sincerely

R Vaughan Williams

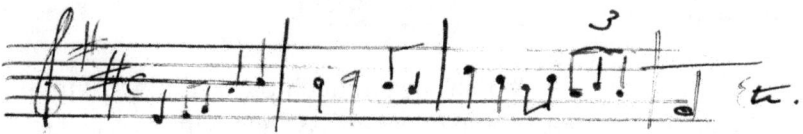

No. 02
To Robert Müller-Hartmann

From R. Vaughan Williams,
The White Gates,
Westcott Road,
Dorking.

Sunday [before September 1939]

Dear Müller-Hartmann

I hear from Genia that you are coming to Craigelly[16] – could we have some time together – I want to know more of your compositions – of which I know shamefully little (your fault chiefly).

Also my wife & I sh^d be so much pleased if Mrs Müller-Hartmann & you both could come & have tea with us one day.

Yours sincerely

R. Vaughan Williams

---

[16] Genia Hornstein; Craigelly was the house of the Hornsteins in Dorking, Surrey.

02

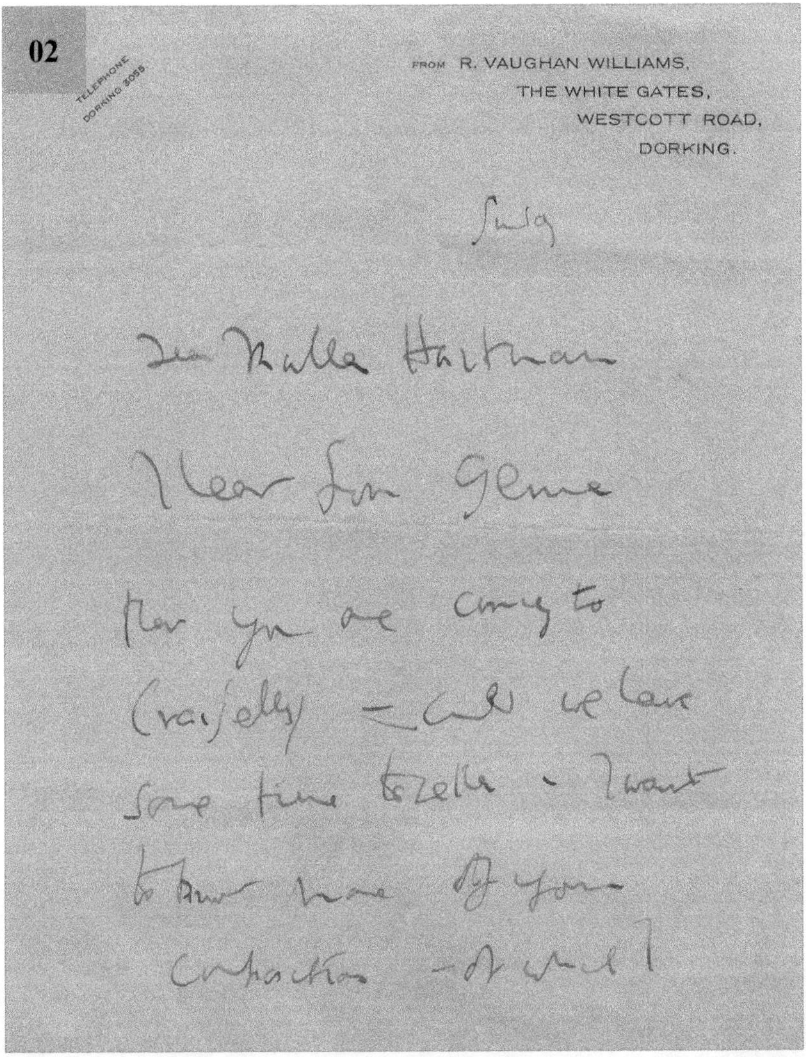
TELEPHONE
DORKING 3055

FROM R. VAUGHAN WILLIAMS,
THE WHITE GATES,
WESTCOTT ROAD,
DORKING.

Sunday

Dear Walter Hartman

I hear from Glenn

that you are coming to

Crayfelly — could we have

some time together — I want

to know more of your

contraption — or what ?

No. 03 [Letter no. 342 in *Letters of Ralph Vaughan Williams*]
To Robert Müller-Hartmann

From R. Vaughan Williams,
The White Gates,
Westcott Road,
Dorking.

Aug 6th 1940

Dear Dr Müller-Hartmann

It was a great pleasure to meet your daughter yesterday – I thought she was looking well though naturally depressed; but I feel that now there is great hope & I cannot but believe for what I think a great wrong will be put right.[17]

I had such pleasure in your lecture at Burchett House[18] the other day. I hope very soon that you will be again able to contribute to our National Culture by your studies in English music.

I feel sure then, in spite of all, you will still continue to believe in English freedom. The Government were in a terrible emergency and had to adopt, all [of] a sudden, whole sale measures which wanted enquiries on many perfectly innocent people – May you soon be free to work for the country of your adoption and for the cause we all have at heart.

Yours sincerely

R. Vaughan Williams

---

[17] Referring to his daughter, Susanne. Müller-Hartmann was interned at a camp on the Isle of Man at this time.
[18] Run by the Dorking & District Refugee Committee.

FROM R. VAUGHAN WILLIAMS,
THE WHITE GATES,
WESTCOTT ROAD,
DORKING.

TELEPHONE
DORKING 3055

Aug 6' 1940

Dear Dr Shulla Hartmann

It was a great pleasure to

meet your daughter yesterday –

I hope she was looking well

& happy actually depressed; but

I feel that now she is grown

better & I cannot lose believe

her than I think a great

way will be past year

I had such pleasure in your lecture
at Burdett House the other day. - I hope
very soon now you will be again
able to contribute to our National
Culture by your studies in English
music

I feel sure too, in whatever field, you
will still continue to believe in English
freedom. No government were in
a terrible emergency than had to
adopt, on a sudden, whole sale measures
which worked unfairly on many perfectly
innocent people - May you again soon
be free to work for the country &
upon all other aims for the cause we all
have at heart

No. 04
To Mrs. Müller-Hartmann

From R. Vaughan Williams,
The White Gates,
Westcott Road,
Dorking.

Sept 6 [1940]

Dear Mrs Müller-Hartmann

Thank you very much for your letter – I do hope your husband will soon get free.[19]

We musicians are trying to prepare a list of interned musicians in case it may be useful.[20]

Would you be so very kind as to fill up the enclosed "questionnaire" and send it to <u>me</u>. It is <u>not</u> going to be used as an application for release (which has already gone in in your case) – But I am using the application form just for convenience.

It was a great pleasure to meet your daughter the other day.

Yours sincerely

R. Vaughan Williams

---

[19] Robert Müller-Hartmann was still interned in a camp on the Isle of Man. He would be released within weeks. See also letter no. 352 in *Letters of Ralph Vaughan Williams* in which Vaughan Williams later wrote to Ursula Wood, "PS Müller-Hartmann is home again."
[20] Vaughan Williams was working on a committee for the Home Office (H.O.) and for the Dorking & District Refugee Committee.

38

FROM R. VAUGHAN WILLIAMS,
THE WHITE GATES,
WESTCOTT ROAD,
DORKING.

TELEPHONE
DORKING 3058

Sep 6

Dear Mr Muller-Hartmann

Thankyou very much for your letter
- I do hope your husband will soon get
free.
We musicians are trying to prepare a
list of interned musicians in

case it may be useful.
Would you be very kind as to fill up the
enclosed "questionnaire" and send it to me
It is not going to be used as an application
for release (and has already gone in in
your case) — But I am using the application
form just for convenience
It was a great pleasure to meet you
and to talk to the one day   yrs sincerely Vaughan Williams

No. 05
To Robert Müller-Hartmann

> From R. Vaughan Williams,
> The White Gates,
> Westcott Road,
> Dorking.

[December 9, 1940 per postmark]

Dear Dr Müller-Hartmann

It is most kind of you to say you will write a <u>critique</u> of the concert next Sunday for the "Dorking Advertizer"[21] – They want about 250 words.

I have pleasure in enclosing two tickets.

> Yours sincerely
>
> R. Vaughan Williams

---

[21] Vaughan Williams seems to consistently misspell "*Dorking Advertiser*". Müller-Hartmann had been released from the camp on the Isle of Man by this time and Vaughan Williams was helping him find work.

Dr Müller Hartmann

Croisell?

Ladygate Road

Dorking

TELEPHONE
DORKING 3068

FROM R. VAUGHAN WILLIAMS,
THE WHITE GATES,
WESTCOTT ROAD,
DORKING.

Dear Dr Müller Hartman

It is most kind of you that you will write
a critique of the concert next Sunday
for the "Dorking Advertiser" — they want
about 250 words.
I have pleasure in enclosing two tickets
Yrs truly
R Vaughan Williams

41

No. 06
To Robert Müller-Hartmann

The White Gates
Dorking

Dec 23 [?1940]

Dear Dr Müller-Hartmann

I hope you recognize your notice in the Dorking Advertizer after Todd & I had worked our wicked will on it!

Thank you so much for writing – it was just right – though of course far too complimentary to one of the composers.

Yours sincerely

R. Vaughan Williams

06

The White Gates
Dorking
Dec 23

Dear Dr Müller-Hartmann

I hope you recognized your
notice in the Dorking Advertiser
after Todd & I had worked
our worked with onit!
Thankyou so much for writing
— it was just right — though
of course far too complimentary
to one of the composers
yrs [?]
R Vaughan Williams

No. 07
To Robert Müller-Hartmann

From R. Vaughan Williams,
The White Gates,
Westcott Road,
Dorking.

[before December 1941][22]

Dear Dr Müller-Hartmann

Thank you very much for the newspaper cuttings – It will give me much pleasure to read them as far as my knowledge of German will permit!

Yours sincerely

R. Vaughan Williams

---

[22] Vaughan Williams is still referring to him as "*Dr.*" Müller-Hartmann.

07

TELEPHONE
DORKING 3055

FROM R. VAUGHAN WILLIAMS,
THE WHITE GATES,
WESTCOTT ROAD,
DORKING.

Dear Dr _Nulle_ Hartman

Thankyou very much for the newspaper
cuttings – It will give me much
pleasure to read them as far as
my knowledge of German will permit.

Yrs _ul_
R Vaughan Williams

No. 08 [Letter no. 308 in *Letters of Ralph Vaughan Williams*]
To Robert Müller-Hartmann

> From R. Vaughan Williams,
> The White Gates,
> Westcott Road,
> Dorking.

Dec 18th [1941 per postmark]

Dear Mr Müller-Hartmann

(Forgive me for making you out an academic!)[23]

I hear that you have written some delightful pianoforte pieces – would you play a short group from them (about 10 minutes) at one of our Wednesday concerts? It would give everyone much pleasure I am sure.

You will probably tell me that you are not a virtuoso pianist – my answer is that I am sure you would play your own music better than anyone else.

May I leave the <u>date</u> doubtful for a short time – it will probably be <u>either</u> Feb 18 or March 4.

> Yours sincerely
>
> R. Vaughan Williams

---

[23] Prior to the date of this letter RVW was under the impression that he was "*Dr.*" Müller-Hartmann. See also Letter No. 10 regarding the concert.

R. Müller Hartmann q
Craisely
Lodge gate Row
Dorking

TELEPHONE
DORKING 3055

FROM R. VAUGHAN WILLIAMS,
THE WHITE GATES,
WESTCOTT ROAD,
DORKING.

Dec 18

Dear Mr Müller-Hartmann
(Forgive me for making you wait on
a committee!)
I hear that you have written some delightful
peaceful piece – would you play a
short extract from them (about 10 minutes)

... or one of our Wednesday concerts?
It would give everyone more pleasure I am
sure.
You will probably tell me that you are not a
virtuoso pianist - my answer is that I
am sure you can play your own music better
than anyone else.
May I leave the date doubtful for a short
time - it will probably be either Feb 18
or March 4   Yours ...
R Vaughan Williams

No. 09
To Robert Müller-Hartmann

[December 26, 1941 per postmark]

Dear Mr Müller-Hartmann

Here is a H.O.[24] letter about Gerson – kindly return it to
me.

Yours sincerely

R. Vaughan Williams

---

[24] Home Office (immigration department). "Gerson" was probably a family
friend or relative. At birth, Robert Müller-Hartmann was named Robert
"Gerson" Müller.

09

R. Müller Hartmann
Craigellen
Ladyegate Row
Dorking

09

Dear Dr. Müller Hartmann
Here is a H.O. letter
about German — kindly
return in time
Yrs very
R Vaughan Williams

No. 10
To Robert Müller-Hartmann

The White Gates
Dorking

Jan 1ˢᵗ [1942]

Dear Mʳ Müller-Hartmann

I think I have arranged for Ruth Dyson[25] to play a short group of your pianoforte pieces at our concert on Wednesday March 4ᵗʰ – will you get into touch direct with her about it?[26]

I hope we can arrange it.

Yours sincerely

R. Vaughan Williams

---

[25] Ruth Dyson was a Dorking pianist and teacher. Müller-Hartmann would later write *Two Bagatelles* for pianoforte and dedicate it to her.
[26] Refer to Letter No. 08 regarding the scheduling of the concert. See also letter no. 376 in *Letters of Ralph Vaughan Williams* in which Vaughan Williams wrote previously to Adine O'Neill asking her to perform at the same concert and describing Robert Müller-Hartmann as "a distinguished German composer".

10

The White Gates
Dorking
Jan 1st

Dear Dr Mills Harrison

I think I have arranged for
Rett Dym to play a short group
of your beautiful pieces
on Concar on Wednesday March 4th
— will you get into touch direct
with her about it?
I hope we can arrange it.

Yrs [?]
R Vaughan Williams

No. 11
To Robert Müller-Hartmann

[?1942-1944]

Dear Mr Müller-Hartmann

I have been asked by the publishers to set the enclosed orchestration to <u>string orchestra</u> (?) "Underlining scherzsism" (!!) – Would you care to undertake it?

The fee the publishers are prepared to pay is £15-0-0.

– By the way the strings should not [be] subdivided too much as the first orchestra which will play it will probably be the Jacques Orchestra[27] which I think is now 4-3-2-2-1.

Yours sincerely

R. Vaughan Williams

---

[27] Founded by Reginald Jacques in 1936. See *Oxford Dictionary of Music*.

11

Dear Miss Horsbrugh

I have been asked by the publisher
to let the enclosed orchestrate
for string orchestra " and any
arrangement (!!) - would you care
to undertake it?
We hear that the publishers can
prepare to pay is £15-0-0

- By the way the strings should not
subdivided too much as to
first orchestra which will play
it will probably be the Jacques
orchestra which I think
no. 6. 3. 2. 2. 1
Yrs sincerely
R Vaughan Williams

55

No. 12
To Robert Müller-Hartmann

The White Gates
Dorking

Oct 16 [?1942-1944]

Dear Mr Müller-Hartmann

Here is still another job! – This time to score the enclosed for <u>strings</u> & <u>organ</u> – The orchestra large but largely good – amateur – the chorus a large body of County Council scholars – There is no necessity to make a special organ part – but just mark the score *CA* or *senza organo* – & mark one of the enclosed copies "Organ Part" & mark it "Tacet" or "play" – My feeling is that with a probably rather weak body of strings & rather huge hall the organ will be wanted most of the time.

I can only squeeze £5-5-0 out of the publishers for this. W^d you care to undertake it? If so it ought to have priority over "Songs of Travel" as it is wanted soon.

Yours sincerely

R. Vaughan Williams

12

The White Gate,
Dorking

Oct 16

Dear Mr Muller Hartman

Here is still another job!
— This time to score
the enclosed for strings
& organ — the orchestra

large but rather
good — amateur — the
chorus a large body

"May" — My feeling
is that with a probably
rather weak body
& strong & fine
huge halls the organ
will be wanted more
of the time.

I can only spend

£5—5—0 out
of the publishers for

P4

W.d you care to undertake it?

If so it ought to
have priority over
"Ships & Travel" as it
is wanted soon
yours

[signature]

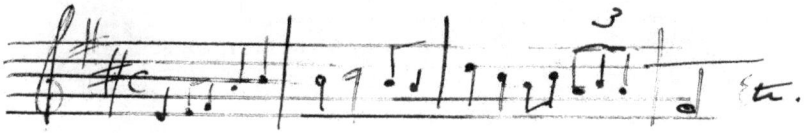

No. 13
To Robert Müller-Hartmann[28]

Dorking

Oct 18 [1942 per postmark]

Dear Mr Müller-Hartmann

Thank you very much for your kind letter & good wishes. We must both bless Dorking & our dear friends the Hornsteins for bringing us together – which has been such a pleasure to me – & as you kindly tell me to you as well.

Yours sincerely

R. Vaughan Williams

---

[28] Susanne Müller-Hartmann, at that time Yanya Hornstein's secretary, had apparently opened the original letter by mistake. The stamp on the transcribed letter is from Jacob (Yanya) Hornstein's company, J. Horn Limited. Probably written as a response to a letter Müller-Hartmann wrote to Vaughan Williams. See *R.V.W.: A Biography of Ralph Vaughan Williams*, p. 252.

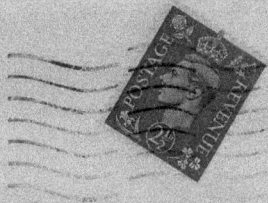

R. Müller Hartmann g
Craigelly
Ledgejata Road
Dorking

Dorking Oct 10

Dear Mr Mike Hartman

Thank you very much for
your kind letter & card wish
we must both thank Dorking
& our dear friends & Hartman
for happy in to thank and
has been a pleasure to
me — I sincerely thank up
to you as well

Yrs sincerely
R Vaughan Williams.

Dorking, Oct. 18.

Dear Mr M-H.

Thank you very much for your kind letter and good wishes. We must both thank Dorking and our dear friends the Hornsteins for bringing us together. It has been such a pleasure to me — and as you kindly tell me to you as well.

Yours sincerely
(Signed) V. W.

Certified true to original
(free of charge)

J. HORN LIMITED
329, HIGH HOLBORN,
LONDON. W.C.1

Temporary Add...
Craigelly, Ladyegate Rd.,
Dorking, Surrey.
Phone 2698.

opened by your daughter

No. 14
To Genia Hornstein from Adeline Vaughan Williams

The White Gates

Friday [?1942 or later]

Dear Genia

Do you think I might venture to ask Mr Müller-Hartmann to glance through a composition that has been sent me from Germany? – A friend of ours Helena Hoven a Russian now married to an Englishman and living in London is very concerned about her niece who is married to a German composer – They are both in a camp for displaced persons in Munich with 2 children and are trying to get to America. Ralph told Helena he could do nothing without some knowledge of the German composer's musical attainments. The result – after long delays – is a thick roll of manuscript (I fear it may be a symphony!)

My friend Helena fled with her parents & niece & nurse during the Russian Revolution. They were first in Malta & then came to England so we have known her & her family off & on for many years.

Ralph always says he can't read a score & if he tried just now it might be the last straw – But you will tell me honestly whether we can venture to ask for help from Mr Müller-Hartmann.

Love from

A. M. Vaughan Williams

Friday - The White Gates

Dear Genia

Do you think I might venture
to ask Mr Müller Hartmann to
glance through a composition that
has been sent me from Germany?
A friend of ours Helena Hoven a
Russian now married to an Englishman
& living in London is very anxious
about her niece who is married to
a German composer — They are both
in a camp for displaced persons in Munich
with 2 children and are trying to get
to America - Ralph told Helena he

could do nothing without some
knowledge of the German composers
musical attainments. The result —
after long delays — is a thick roll
of manuscript! (I fear it may be a
Symphony!)
My friend Helena fled with her
parents & niece & nurse during
the Russian revolution. They were
first in Malta & then came to
England so we have known her &
her family off & on for many years.
Ralph always says he can't read a
score & if he tried just now it
might be the last straw — But you
will tell me honestly whether we
can venture to ask for help from
Mr Müller Hartmann — Love from
A.M. Vaughan Williams

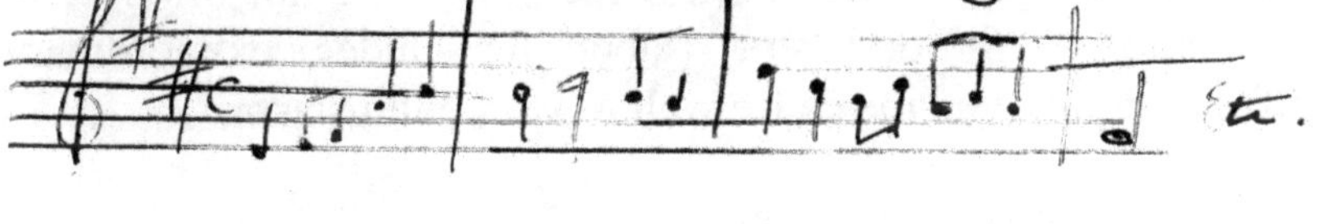
Etc.

No. 15
To Robert Müller-Hartmann

From R. Vaughan Williams,
The White Gates,
Westcott Road,
Dorking.

April 11 [1943 per postmark]

Dear Mr Müller-Hartmann

Thank you very much for your discerning & discriminating but kind & encouraging notice of the 'Passion'[29] – I know that the chorus knew their work thoroughly and love it – & that can go very far even if the voices are not first rate & the soloists & orchestra (labouring under extraordinary difficulties) served the cause well & with enthusiasm.

Thank you once again.

Yours sincerely

R. Vaughan Williams

---

[29] Vaughan Williams conducted community performances of Bach's *St. Matthew Passion* in Dorking almost every year. Müller-Hartmann had probably written a review in the *Dorking Advertiser*.

15

R. Muller Hartman?
Craigells
Ladyegate Road
Dorking

15

TELEPHONE
DORKING 3055

FROM R. VAUGHAN WILLIAMS,
THE WHITE GATES,
WESTCOTT ROAD,
DORKING.

April 11

Dear Mr Miller-Hartman

Thankyou very much for your
obscurity & discernment in
kind & encouragy some of the
passion - I know him to close
knew their work roughly and love

71

No. 16
To Robert Müller-Hartmann

From R. Vaughan Williams,
The White Gates,
Westcott Road,
Dorking.

July 14, 1943

Dear Mr Müller-Hartmann

I am so sorry I was prevented from listening in to your orchestration – But Genia tells me that it sounded lovely.[30]

Thank you very much.

Yours sincerely

R. Vaughan Williams

---

[30] Possibly a work by Müller-Hartmann broadcast on the radio.

16

DORKING
12 15PM
15 JLY
1943
SURREY

TWO PENCE HALF PENNY

R. Müller Hartmann
Craiselly
Longesete Road
Dorking

16

TELEPHONE
DORKING 3055

FROM R. VAUGHAN WILLIAMS,
THE WHITE GATES,
WESTCOTT ROAD,
DORKING.

July 14 1943

Dear Dr Müller-Hartman

I am so sorry I was prevented
from listening in to your orchestration
— But Genia tells me part is someone

your Vaughan Williams

No. 17
To Susanne Müller-Hartmann

From R. Vaughan Williams,
The White Gates,
Westcott Road,
Dorking.

Sep 1st [1943 per postmark]

My Dear Suzanne

Thank you so much for the beautiful copies. It has helped me a lot.

Love from Uncle Ralph

17

Miss Luella Hartner
Craigellen
Ladygate Row
Dorking

17

FROM R. VAUGHAN WILLIAMS,
THE WHITE GATES,
WESTCOTT ROAD,
DORKING.

TELEPHONE
DORKING 3055

My Dear Suzanne
thankyou so much for the beautiful
calendar — It has helped me a
lot   love fm Uncle Ralph

No. 18
To Robert Müller-Hartmann[31]

The White Gates

April 23 [1944 per calendar]

Dear Müller-Hartmann

I'm so glad you both can come – Please be at the Ballerina Restaurant[32] Tuesday May 9 at 6. pm. Day clothes of course.

Here are the tickets.

Yours sincerely

R. Vaughan Williams

---

[31] In the hand of Adeline Vaughan Williams, signed by RVW.
[32] Probably the restaurant on Rosebery Ave. near Sadler's Wells Theatre.

18

The White Gates

April 23

Dear Müller Hartmann
I'm so glad you both
can come – Please be at
the Ballerina restaurant
Tuesday May 9 at 6o pm.
Day clothes of course
Here are the tickets

Yrs
A Vaughan Williams

No. 19
To the Churchwarden c/o R. Müller-Hartmann

From R. Vaughan Williams,
The White Gates,
Westcott Road,
Dorking.

May 4th [1944 per postmark]

To the Churchwarden

Please keep a good seat for Mr Hartmann as he is writing the notice for the "Dorking Advertizer".

R. Vaughan Williams

19

R. *Mila Hartman*

S. T. Houston ?

Craigelly

Ladyegate Road

Deepdene   *Dorking*

19

TELEPHONE
DORKING 3005

FROM R. VAUGHAN WILLIAMS,
THE WHITE GATES,
WESTCOTT ROAD,
DORKING.

May 4

To the churchwarden

Please keep a few seats for Mr
Hartman & be 5 writing.
be voice for the 'Dorking advertiser'

R Vaughan Williams

No. 20
To Robert Müller-Hartmann

The White Gates
Dorking

May 16th [1944 per postmark]

Dear Mr Müller-Hartmann

Thank you very much for your kind and stimulating notice in the Dorking Advertizer – I am very grateful to you.

Yours sincerely

R. Vaughan Williams

R. McMc Hartram ?
Clr Y. Humstein ?
Craigelly
    Ludgegate Road
        Dorking

No Whitegates
Darley
May 16th

Dear mr Müller Hartman

Thankyou very much
for your kind and
stimulating article
in the Darley advertiser
— I am very grateful
to you
Yours sincerely
R Vaughan Williams

No. 21 [Letter no. 439 in *Letters of Ralph Vaughan Williams*]
To Robert Müller-Hartmann

> From R. Vaughan Williams,
> The White Gates,
> Westcott Road,
> Dorking.

Jan 2ⁿᵈ 1945

Dear Mʳ Müller-Hartmann

    I do not know whether you would care to undertake a task which is chiefly copying – but involves a certain amount of scholarship. It is no less than to copy out the voice parts of Bach's Mass in B minor in the most correct edition available.

    I have been preparing a version of the mass adapted to the English liturgy. – So in addition to all you would have to decipher my rough notes! – Though this is not really so formidable since you would get the notes from the printed copy & as to the words you could check my hieroglyphics from a printed prayer book.

    There is no hurry about the work as there is no chance of it being printed till after the war. I could lend you a B.G. and a Novello copy corrected.[33]

    Would you care to undertake it? I suggest as a preliminary a fee of £50-0-0 – which could be adjusted later.

> Yours sincerely
>
> R. Vaughan Williams

---

[33] Bach Gesellschaft edition and Novello and Co., music publishers.

21

R. Müller Hartmann
Craigells
Ladygate Road
Dorking

21

TELEPHONE
DORKING 3056

FROM R. VAUGHAN WILLIAMS,
THE WHITE GATES,
WESTCOTT ROAD,
DORKING.

Jan 2nd 1945

Dear Mr Müller Hartmann

I do not know whether you would care
to undertake a task which is chiefly
copying – but involves a certain
amount of scholarship. It is no

less than to copy out the voice parts of [the] Bach Mass in B minor in the most correct edition available.

I have been preparing a version of the mass adapted to the English Liturgy. So in addition to all this you would have to decipher my rough notes! — Though this is not really so formidable

From R. Vaughan Williams,
The White Gates,
Westcott Road,
Dorking.
Telephone Dorking 1055

2

FROM R. VAUGHAN WILLIAMS,
THE WHITE GATES,
WESTCOTT ROAD,
DORKING.
TELEPHONE
DORKING 1055

since you would get the notes from the printed copy & as to the words you can check my hieroglyphics from a printed prayer book.

There is no hurry about the work

as there is no chance of it being
printed till after war
I could lend you a B.g. and a
Novello copy corrected.
Would you care to undertake it?
I suggest as a preliminary a
fee of £50-0-0 — and I could

TELEPHONE
DORKING 2055
FROM R. VAUGHAN WILLIAMS,
THE WHITE GATES,
WESTCOTT ROAD,
DORKING.

be of... later
Yrs
R Vaughan Williams

No. 22
To Robert Müller-Hartmann

The White Gates
Dorking

Jan 4th [1945 per postmark]

Dear Müller-Hartmann

(May we stop this "mistering" and "doctoring")[34]

It is splendid of you to be willing to do this[35] – what about Monday afternoon about 2.30 – then we could have a cup of tea about 4.15 & go on after if necessary.

I am also free Tuesday if Monday does not suit you.

Yours sincerely

R. Vaughan Williams

---

[34] Müller-Hartmann had probably been addressing Vaughan Williams as "*Dr.*" Vaughan Williams; prior to December 18, 1941, Vaughan Williams had been addressing Robert Müller-Hartmann as "*Dr.* Müller-Hartmann" and thereafter as "*Mr. Müller-Hartmann*". See Letter No. 08.
[35] Vaughan Williams had asked him to copy the voice parts of Bach's Mass in B minor.

R. Miller Hartman Q
Craigella
Ladygate Road
Dorking

The White Gates
Dorking
Jan 4

Dear Miller Hartman
(may we stop this "mistering"
& "doctoring")
It is pleasant & you kindly
booked
— we come Monday
afternoon about 2.30
— then we could have a
cup of tea about 4.15

& go on after it necessary

I am also free Tuesday
if Monday does not
suit you

Yours very
A Vaughan Williams

No. 23
To Robert Müller-Hartmann

[January 1945 or later]

Dear Müller-Hartmann

Here are the choruses of the "B minor" – Full of mistakes as the 'artist' who did the writing was not a musician.[36]

Yrs

R. Vaughan Williams

---

[36] Referring to himself, of course.

23

Dear Millie Horton

Here are the climax of
the "Browne" — first
2 sketches = the
'action' who do the
unity was 2 or e
[illegible]

R Vaughan Williams

No. 24
To Robert Müller-Hartmann

The White Gates
Dorking

[January 1945 or later]

Dear Müller-Hartmann

I am sorry for the delay in finishing up about the B minor Mass.

We arranged I think for £50-0-0 & that was to include one or two 'realisations' of the <u>continuo</u> later on.

I have not yet found a copyist to make the second copy – they all seem to be busy. I have much pleasure in enclosing a cheque – & I hope you feel that this is all correct.

Yours sincerely

R. Vaughan Williams

24

The wholesale
Dairy

Dear Miller Hartman

I am sorry for the
delay in finishing
what about ... B. ...

... ... I felt
be aware

to $ 50 -... ...
... ... to include
one or two realisations

of the continues later

on.
I have not yet found
a copyist to make
the second copy — they
all seem to be busy
. I have much pleasure
~~duly~~ enclosing a
cheque — I I hope
you feel ~~that~~ this
is all correct

Yrs aff
A Vaughan Williams

No. 25
To Robert Müller-Hartmann

From R. Vaughan Williams,
The White Gates,
Westcott Road,
Dorking.

[January 1945 or later]

Dear Müller-Hartmann

I appreciate your praise as always – perhaps one day a whole work will grow out of them. The bells & trombones were to have been louder & further off – The trumpets sounded like cornets. But I thought the singing was excellent.

Yrs

R. Vaughan Williams

25

TELEPHONE
DORKING 3055.

FROM R. VAUGHAN WILLIAMS,
THE WHITE GATES,
WESTCOTT ROAD,
DORKING.

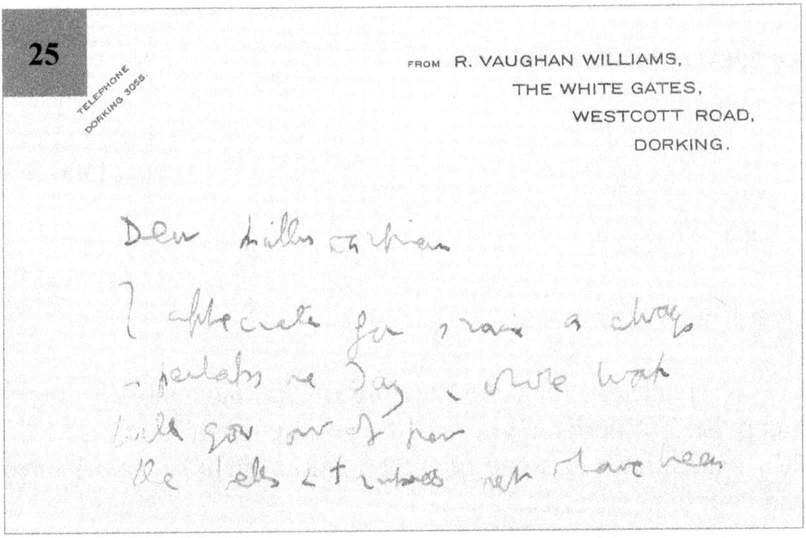

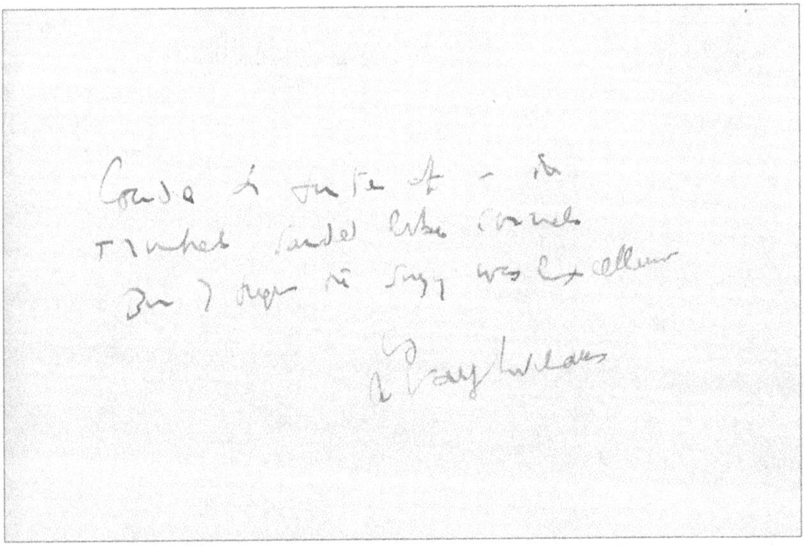

Dear [illegible]

I appreciate your making a change
– perhaps the [illegible] whole work
[illegible] gone out of [illegible]
the [illegible] & trumpets [illegible] have been

Could [illegible] of it – the
trumpet sounded like cornets
But I agree the singing was excellent

Yrs
R Vaughan Williams

No. 26
To Robert Müller-Hartmann[37]

The White Gates
Dorking

April 18 [?1945]

Dear Müller-Hartmann

    Thank you for your generous offer. I have already found a copyist, but perhaps you will be good enough later on to do the "realization" of some of the continuo for me – also I have had your expert advice.

Yours sincerely

R. Vaughan Williams

---

[37] In the hand of Adeline Vaughan Williams, signed by RVW.

The White Gates
Dorking
April 18

Dear Müller Hartmann

Thank you for your generous
offer. I have already found a
copyist, but perhaps you will be
good enough later on to do the
"realization" of some of the
Continuos for me — Also I have
had your expert advice.

Yours sincerely
R. Vaughan Williams

No. 27
To Robert Müller-Hartmann

From R. Vaughan Williams,
The White Gates,
Westcott Road,
Dorking.

May 20 [?1945]

Dear Müller-Hartmann

  I have been consulting the Authors' Society & they are of opinion that I have only realized by half the material value of your work. I have been through the score again & seeing more fully the skills, knowledge & mental concentration also the <u>creative</u> effort contained in it that they are quite right.

  I fear it is now too late to undo my quite unwitting discourtesy – but I hope that the enclosed "scrap of paper" will at all events technically salve my conscience.[38]

  With revered thanks.

Yours very sincerely

R. Vaughan Williams

---

[38] Perhaps referring to Müller-Hartmann's work on the B minor Mass and probably including a check for additional money.

FROM R. VAUGHAN WILLIAMS,
THE WHITE GATES,
WESTCOTT ROAD,
DORKING.

TELEPHONE
DORKING 3055

May 20

Dear Müller-Hartman

I have been consulting
the authors society & they
are of opinion that I
have only realized ½
half the material value
of your work. I have been
through the score again &
realize more fully the

still, knowledge of mental concentration also the creative effort contained in it then they are such now.

I fear it is now too late to undo my quite unwitting discourtesy – but I hope that the enclosed "scrap of paper" will at all events technically salve my conscience.

With renewed thanks

Yours very truly

R Vaughan Williams

No. 28
To Robert Müller-Hartmann

Dorking

June 5 [?1945]

Dear Müller-Hartmann

     Here is a preface for B minor – if you approve will you add your signature.

Yrs

R. Vaughan Williams

28

Darling
Tues

Dear Nulla Hartman

Here is a preface
for Brian

— if you altera well
ye and you rejections

Vaughnblum

No. 29
To Robert Müller-Hartmann

The White Gates
Dorking

Nov 3 [?1945 or later]

Dear Müller-Hartmann

So far as I can make out the complicated "union" rules, I owe you the enclosed.

Please accept it, not indeed as representing in any way the value of your ~~wise counsel & help~~ wisdom whose price is, indeed, above rubies but as the only tangible expression I can give of my gratitude & satisfaction that so distinguished a musician as yourself should be willing to place his skill and experience at my disposal.

Yrs

R. Vaughan Williams

29

The White Gates
Dorking
Nov 3

Dear ~~Dear~~ Müller-Hartmann

So far as I can make out
the complicated "union" rules, I
owe you the enclose[d]

please accept it, nor indeed as
representing in any way the value
of you ~~this~~ ~~counsel~~ ~~that~~ wisdom whose
price is, indeed, above rubies.

her as the only tangible expression
I can give of my gratitude
& satisfaction that so distinguished
a musician as yourself should
be willing to place his skill
and experience at my disposal

yrs A Vaughan Williams

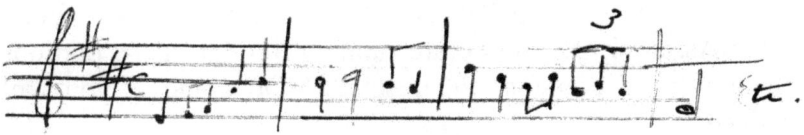

No. 30
To Robert Müller-Hartmann

The White Gates
Dorking

Nov 1 [1946 per calendar]

Dear Müller-Hartmann

Thank you very much for your letter[39] – I think your evidence is conclusive – Any how for the purposes of my privately printed copies I had to use the Novello[40] version as it stood.

By the way on Sat: Nov 23 at 3.0 p.m. at the White Horse Assembly Room we are running through those portions which we are doing at the festival.[41] Do come if you feel inclined.

Yrs

R. Vaughan Williams

---

[39] Probably again referring to the B minor Mass. Müller-Hartmann had written earlier about some textual discrepancies between the Bach Gesellschaft edition and the autograph.

[40] Novello and Co., music publishers. See letter no. 452 in *Letters of Ralph Vaughan Williams* for a very interesting note about Vaughan Williams's thoughts on his English version of Bach's Mass in B minor.

[41] The White Horse Hotel in Dorking dates from the late 13th century; referring to a future performance at the Leith Hill Musical Festival.

30

The Midgate
Derry
Nov 1

Dear Miller Hartram

Many thanks for
your letter – I have
your evidence,
conclusion – any
law for the purposes
of any private friends

Chris I hope to make Novello version as in Score

By the way on Sat: Nov 23 at 3.0 P.m at the White Horse Assembly Room we are running those little parties while we are doing our festival. Do come in if you feel inclined

R Vaughan Williams

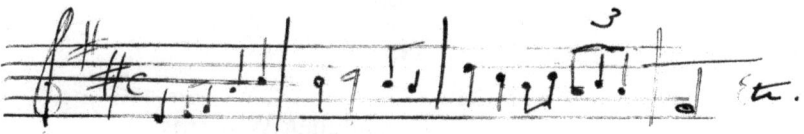

No. 31
To Robert Müller-Hartmann

From R. Vaughan Williams,
The White Gates,
Westcott Road,
Dorking.

[?1946 or later]

Dear Müller-Hartmann

Please use my name whenever you wish. Thank you very much for the information about "Job" – I am so glad you are coming to "Sir John".[42]

Yrs

R. Vaughan Williams

---

[42] *Job, a Masque for Dancing* and *Sir John in Love*.

31

FROM R. VAUGHAN WILLIAMS,
THE WHITE GATES,
WESTCOTT ROAD,
DORKING.

TELEPHONE
DORKING 3055

Dear Müller-Hartmann

Please use my name whenever you will
& perhaps it would for the information about
"Tod" — I am so glad you are
coming to "Sir John"

& R Vaughan Williams

No. 32
To Robert Müller-Hartmann

The White Gates
Dorking

[April 23, 1947 per postmark]

Dear Müller-Hartmann

I am so glad you were able to come – I appreciate your praise very much. It w^d be false modesty if I did not think that the chorus really deserved it.[43]

Yrs

R. Vaughan Williams

I hope you were not shocked at the trombones!

---

[43] Refers to the concert on April 18, 1947, at the Leith Hill Musical Festival in Dorking; Vaughan Williams's English version of Bach's B minor Mass was finally performed.

R. Mala Hertram P.

Craizell

Langgate Road,

Dorking

Leithhill Festival
April 1947

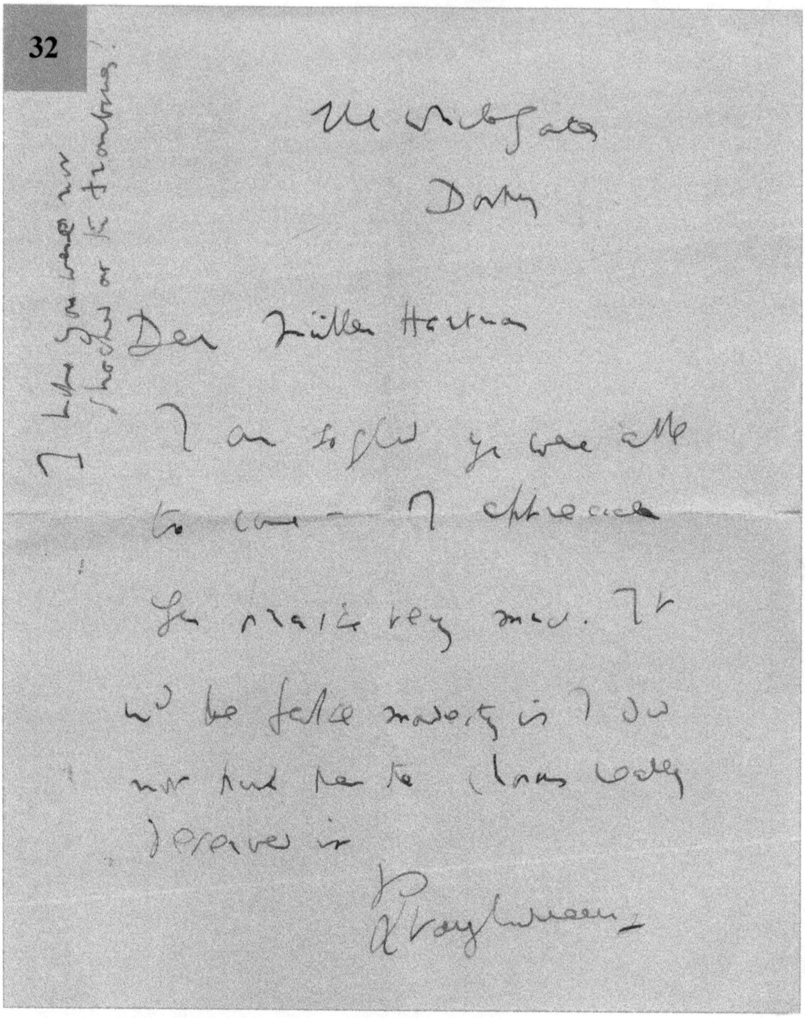

The Delegates
Derby

Dear [illegible] Hartman

I am so glad you were able
to come. I appreciate

[illegible] very much. It
will be felt [illegible] as I do
not find [illegible] [illegible]
[illegible]

[illegible signature]

[left margin, vertical: I hope you [illegible] [illegible] [illegible] or its troubles.]

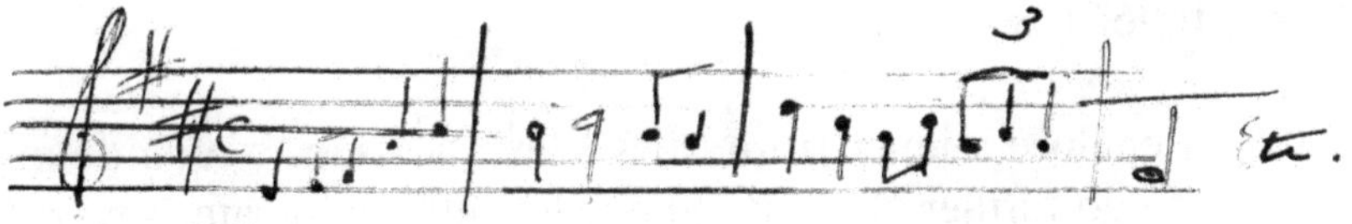
Etc.

No. 33
To Robert Müller-Hartmann

From R. Vaughan Williams,
The White Gates,
Westcott Road,
Dorking.

7th August, 1947.

R. Müller-Hartmann, Esq.,
Craigelly,
Ladyegate Road,
DORKING.

Dear Müller-Hartmann,

I enclose a letter from Miss May Harrison.[44] Would you like me to go further about it? She is herself a first-rate player. I do not know her sister's playing but I suppose that she would not play with anyone unworthy.

Yours sincerely,

R. Vaughan Williams

Enc.

---

[44] Violinist (1891-1959) and sister of Beatrice, the cellist, who gave the first radio performance of Elgar's *Cello Concerto*, and Margaret, a pianist, and least well known of the three. See *Oxford Dictionary of Music*.

33

From R. VAUGHAN WILLIAMS,
THE WHITE GATES,
WESTCOTT ROAD,
DORKING.

7th August, 1947.

R. Muller-Hartmann, Esq.,
    Craigelly,
        Ladyegate Road,
           DORKING.

Dear Müller-Hartmann,

    I enclose a letter from Miss May Harrison.
Would you like me to go further about it?   She is
herself a first-rate player.   I do not know her
sister's playing but I suppose that she would not
play with anyone unworthy.

             Yours sincerely,

             R. VAUGHAN WILLIAMS.

Enc.

No. 34 [Letter no. 481 in *Letters of Ralph Vaughan Williams*]
To Robert Müller-Hartmann

The White Gates,
Westcott Road,
Dorking.

14th August, 1947.

Dear Müller-Hartmann

I am so glad you like the idea of May Harrison playing your work. I think it would be nice if you wrote to her yourself, here is her address

647 Nell Gwyn House,
Sloane Avenue,
London. S.W.3.

Meanwhile there is something I should like you to do for me if you feel inclined. The young man who writes my music for me[45] is at present away on holiday, will you do it? what I want you to do is to correct any mistakes before I send it to the copyist and also tell me of any places where you think I have made any error of judgment. The work is a suite for string orchestra. I should be very grateful if you would do this for me.[46]

Yrs

R. Vaughan Williams

p.s. My usual typist is away!

---

[45] Referring to Roy Douglas.
[46] Referring to *Partita for Double String Orchestra,* a re-working of the 1938 *Double Trio* for string sextet. The *Partita* was later dedicated to Robert Müller-Hartmann. See *R.V.W.: A Biography of Ralph Vaughan Williams,* p. 277 and *A Catalogue of the Works of Ralph Vaughan Williams,* p. 163.

34

The White Gates
Westcott ~~Street,~~ Row
Dorking.

14th August, 1947.

Dear Zillah-Hartman

    I am so glad you like the idea of May Harrison
playing your work. I think it would be nice if
you wrote to her yourself, here is her address

      647 Nell Gwyn House,
      Sloane Avenue,
      London S.W.3.

    Meanwhile there is something I should like
you to do for me if you feel inclined. The young
man who writes my music for me is at present away
on holiday, will you do it? what I want you to do
is to correct any mistakes before I send it to the
copyist and also tell me of any places where you
think I have made any eror of judgment. The
work is a suite for string orchestra. I should
be very grateful if you would do this for me.

        yo R Vaughan williams

        R. Vaughan Williams.

P.t. My usual typsor is away!

127

No. 35
To Robert Müller-Hartmann

The White Gates,
Dorking.

November, 1947.

Dear Müller-Hartmann

Sir Adrian Boult will rehearse my new Symphony from 10.30 to 1.30 at Maida Vale Studio on Tuesday, December 16th.[47]

Is there any chance that Mrs Müller-Hartmann & you could come?

Yours sincerely

R. Vaughan Williams

If so I will send you 2 tickets

---

[47] Referring to Symphony No. 6 in E minor.

35

The White Gates,

Dorking.

November, 1947.

Dear Mulle Hawthorne

    Sir Adrian Boult will rehearse my new
Symphony from 10.30 to 1.30 at Maida Vale Studio on
Tuesday, December 16th.   Mr Mille Hawthorne

    Is there any chance that you could come?

    Yours sincerely,

    R Vaughan Williams

    (R. Vaughan Williams).

I will send 2 tickets.

No. 36
To Robert Müller-Hartmann[48]

The White Gates,
Dorking,

27th December, 1947.

Dear Müller-Hartmann

Thank you very much. I can say no more, but you know how I value your good opinion.

Yrs

R. Vaughan Williams

R. Müller-Hartmann, Esq.

---

[48] Written in response to a letter Müller-Hartmann had written on December 16, 1947, which explained that he left the studio rehearsal of Symphony No. 6 in E minor without speaking to Vaughan Williams because of his emotional reaction: "I never anticipated the overwhelming impression the real thing would make on me." He further mentioned he thought the new symphony transcended Symphony No. 4 in F minor and Symphony No. 5 in D major. See also *R.V.W.: A Biography of Ralph Vaughan Williams*, p. 279 and *The Works of Ralph Vaughan Williams*, pp. 300-1.

36

The White Gates,
Dorking,

27th December, 1947.

De Müller-Hartmann

Thank you very much.   I can say no more,
but you know how I value your good opinion.

W R Vaughan Williams

(R. Vaughan Williams).

R. Müller Hartmann, Esq.

No. 37
To Robert Müller-Hartmann

The White Gates,
Dorking,

12th March, 1948.

Dear Müller-Hartmann

I should be delighted if you and Mrs. Müller-Hartmann could come to rehearsals and performance of my "Partita".[49] The rehearsals are probably Friday March 19th. 10.30 and March 20th 4 o'clock. There is a performance I understand both on the 20th and 21st.

I am sorry the "News Chronicle" worried you, but I think they were fairly harmless as things go. Of course they were incorrect, but then the Press is never correct.

I am asking Mrs. Beckett[50] to send you tickets for rehearsals and performance.

Yrs

R. Vaughan Williams

Robert Müller-Hartmann, Esq.
68b, Belsize Park Gardens,
London, N.W.3

---

[49] *Partita for Double String Orchestra*. Müller-Hartmann helped with its reworking and Vaughan Williams dedicated the work to him. The work was first performed by the BBC Symphony Orchestra, conducted by Sir Adrian Boult, on March 20, 1948 (see *A Catalogue of the Works of Ralph Vaughan Williams*, p. 163). Adeline Vaughan Williams and Müller-Hartmann listened to the broadcast (see *R.V.W.: A Biography of Ralph Vaughan Williams*, pp. 282-3).

[50] Mrs. Beckett was Sir Adrian Boult's secretary.

37

The White Gates,
Dorking,

12th March, 1948.

Dear Müller Hartmann

I should be delighted if you and Mrs. Müller-Hartmann could come to rehearsals and performance of my "Partita". The rehearsals are probably Friday March 19th. 10.30 and March 20th 4 o'clock. There is a performance I understand both on the 20th and 21st.

I am sorry the "News Chronicle" worried you, but I think they were fairly harmless as things go. Of course they were incorrect, but then the Press is never correct.

I amasking Mrs. Beckett to send you tickets for rehearsals and performance.

Yrs R Vaughan Williams

(R. Vaughan Williams).

Robert Müller-Hartmann, Esq.
68b, Belsize Park Gardens,
London, N.W.3

No. 38
To Robert Müller-Hartmann[51]

The White Gates,
Dorking,

25th March, 1948.

Dear Müller-Hartmann

Thank you so much for writing. I value your appreciation very much

I have not yet heard from Curwen's[52], but I think we can go ahead with the translation.

Yrs

R. Vaughan Williams

R. Müller-Hartmann, Esq.
68 B. Belsize Park Gardens,
London, N.W.3.

---

[51] Written in response to a letter Müller-Hartmann had written to Vaughan Williams on March 21, 1948 in which he expressed his pleasure from hearing the radio broadcast of *Partita for Double String Orchestra* and his thanks for having the work dedicated to him. Müller-Hartmann also mentioned that he would soon begin his work on the German translation of *Sancta Civitas.*

[52] Music publisher J. Curwen and Sons, publisher of *Sancta Civitas* and other works by Vaughan Williams.

38

The White Gates,
Dorking,

25th March, 1948.

De Müller Hartman

Thank you so much for writing.   I value
your appreciation very much

I have not yet heard from Curwen's, but I
think we can go ahead with the translation.

(R. Vaughan Williams).

R. Müller-Hartmann, Esq.
68 B. Belsize Park Gardens,
London, N.W.3.

No. 39
To Robert Müller-Hartmann[53]

The White Gates,
Dorking,

May 22nd. 1948.

Dear Müller-Hartmann

    I feel it a great honour to be able to claim you as a fellow citizen. I am glad to hear that you are doing a good deal of work for the B.B.C..

    I found the missing page of the Symphony alright.

    My affectionate greetings to Mrs M. H. & Susanne

Yrs

RVW

Robert Müller-Hartmann, Esq.,
Craigelly,
Ladygate Road, DORKING.

---

[53] See *R.V.W.: A Biography of Ralph Vaughan Williams*, p. 283.

39

The White Gates,
Dorking,

May 22nd. 1948.

Dear Miller Hartman

I feel it a great honour to be able to
claim you as a fellow citizen.   I am glad to hear
that you are doing a good deal of work for the
B.B.C..

I found the missing page of the Symphony
alright.

my affectionate greetings to mrs R.H.
& Susanne

(R. Vaughan Williams).

Robert Müller-Hartmann, Esq.,
Craigelly,
Ladygate Road,   DORKING.

No. 40
To Robert Müller-Hartmann[54]

From R. Vaughan Williams,
The White Gates,
Westcott Road,
Dorking.

Sunday [?1948 or later]

Dear Müller-Hartmann

I listened on Wednesday – I thought your piece sounded delightful – I envied the skill! – As far as I could judge it was a good performance and came well over the air.

I hope we shall hear it again soon.

Yrs

R. Vaughan Williams

---

[54] The work by Müller-Hartmann is not determined.

40

FROM **R. VAUGHAN WILLIAMS,**
THE WHITE GATES,
WESTCOTT ROAD,
DORKING.

TELEPHONE
DORKING 3055

Sunday

Dear Müller-Hartmann

I listened on Wednesday
- I hope you received
something delightful -
I envied the skill!
- As far as I could
judge in one & one
performance and some

with over the air

I hope we shall learn
again soon

Yours
R Vaughan Williams

No. 41
To Robert Müller-Hartmann[55]

The White Gates

May 29 [?1948]

Dear Müller-Hartmann

I enclose a letter from Leslie Boosey[56] to May Harrison which you may like to read.

Yrs

R. Vaughan Williams

---

[55] In the hand of Adeline Vaughan Williams, signed by RVW. [See Letters No. 33 and No. 44 concerning May Harrison]
[56] Boosey & Hawkes, Ltd., music publishers.

41

The White Gates
May 29 —

Dear Müller Hartmann
I enclose a letter from
Leslie Boosey to May Harrison
which you may like to read.

R Vaughan Williams

No. 42
To Robert Müller-Hartmann

The White Gates

Sep 27 [?1948 or later][57]

Dear Müller-Hartmann

I hear the BBC (Manchester) are doing my Partita for Orchestra.

I have to confess that I did not accept all your corrections – but in one case I wrote the passage again.

Yrs

R. Vaughan Williams

---

[57] Certainly after the first performance of *Partita for Double String Orchestra* on March 20, 1948, and likely shortly after the first *public* performance on July 29, 1948. See *A Catalogue of the Works of Ralph Vaughan Williams*, p. 163.

42

The White Gates

Feb 27

Dear Nick Hartmann

I hear that the BBC
(Manchester) are doing my
Partita on October

I have to confess that
I did not correct all your
corrections — but in any
case I wrote to Lawrence
again yrs

R Vaughan Williams

No. 43
To Mrs. Müller-Hartmann from Adeline Vaughan Williams

The White Gates

January 4 [1949]

Dear Mrs Müller-Hartmann

I would like to tell you how much pleasure I am getting from the lovely azalea you sent us – I feel I ought to have sent a very special message to you and I let Mr Müller-Hartmann go without it – I only hope the lovely little bush will thrive – at present it is well and is putting out fresh blossoms – Thank you very much for it –

With all good wishes for 1949 from us both –

Yours sincerely

Adeline Vaughan Williams

43

The White Gates
January 4

Dear Mrs Müller Hartmann

I would like to tell you
how much pleasure I am
getting from the lovely Azalea
you sent us — I feel I ought
to have sent a very special
message to you and I let
Dr Müller Hartmann go without
it — I only hope the lovely
little bush will thrive — at
present it is well and is pulling
out fresh blossoms — Thank you

very much for it —
with all good wishes
for 1949 from us both —
Yours sincerely
Adeline Vaughan Williams

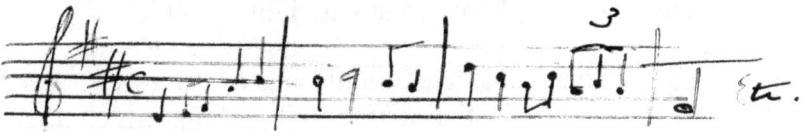

No. 44
To Robert Müller-Hartmann[58]

The White Gates,
Dorking,

17th February, 1949.

Dear Müller-Hartmann,

I wonder if you would consider making a German translation of my Opera "Pilgrim's Progress". There is no performance, alas, in view, but I think a German translation might possibly lead to a performance abroad.

Will you let me know what you think about it?

A lot of the words are straight out of "Bunyan", and I think there is already an existing translation of that which might help you; and a lot is out of the Bible.

Yrs

R. Vaughan Williams

R. Müller-Hartmann, Esq.,
Craigelly,
Ladygate Road, Dorking.

---

[58] See also *R.V.W.: A Biography of Ralph Vaughan Williams*, pp. 288-9.

44

The White Gates,
Dorking,

17th February, 1949.

Dear Müller Hartmann,

I wonder if you would consider making
a German translation of my Opera "Pilgrim's
Progress".   There is no performance, alas, in
view, but I think a German translation might
possibly lead to a performance abroad.

Will you let me know what you think about
it?

A lot of the words are straight out of
"Bunyan", and I think there is already an existing
translation of that which might help you; and a
lot is out of the Bible.

(R. Vaughan Williams).

R. Müller Hartmann, Esq.,
Craigelly,
Ladygate Road,   Dorking.

No. 45
To Robert Müller-Hartmann

The White Gates,
Dorking, SURREY.

2nd. November, 1949.

Dear Müller-Hartmann

On Sunday, November 20th at 3.30 p.m. some singers and players are coming here to let me hear a "try through" of two new works of mine.[59]

Would you care to come and hear them? My space is so limited that I can only ask a very few but I should like you to be among them.

Yrs

R. Vaughan Williams

R. Mueller Hartmann, Esq.,
c/o J. Hornstein, Esq.,
Craigelly,
Ladyegate Road, Dorking.

---

[59] *An Oxford Elegy* and *Fantasia (Quasi Variazione) on the 'Old 104ᵗʰ' Psalm Tune*. See *A Catalogue of the Works of Ralph Vaughan Williams*, pp. 187-8 for extensive details about these first performances at The White Gates. See also *R.V.W.: A Biography of Ralph Vaughan Williams*, p. 297 for other details and a similar invitation written to long-time friend Isidore Schwiller.

45

The White Gates,
Dorking, SURREY.

2nd. November, 1949.

Dear ~~Mülle Hartmann~~

On Sunday, November 20th at 2.30 p.m.
some singers and players are coming here to let
me hear a "try through" of two new works of mine.

Would you care to come and hear them?
My space is so limited that I can only ask a very
few but I should like you to be among them.

R Vaughan Williams

(R. Vaughan Williams).

R. Mueller Hartmann, Esq.,
c/o J. Hornstein, Esq.,
Craigelly,
Ladyegate Road,   Dorking.

No. 46
To Robert Müller-Hartmann

The White Gates,
Dorking, SURREY.

9th November, 1949.

Dear Müller-Hartmann

I am so glad you can come on the 20th.

Do read the "Scholar Gipsy" and "Thyrsis" which comes next to it in the book.[60]

As regards the 104th Psalm you need not read that except for the pleasure of reading such magnificent language. My "Fantasia" is on the <u>tune</u> of the metrical version of the 104th Psalm in Sternhold & Hopkins[61] and I only used one or two verses for the sake of giving the choir something to sing.

Yrs

R. Vaughan Williams

R. Mueller Hartmann, Esq.,
c/o J. Hornstein, Esq.,
Craigelly,
Ladyegate Road, Dorking.

---

[60] The two poems by Matthew Arnold from which Vaughan Williams drew the text for *An Oxford Elegy*. See *A Catalogue of the Works of Ralph Vaughan Williams*, p. 187.

[61] Probably *The Whole Booke of Psalmes, Collected into English metre, by Thomas Sternhold, John Hopkins, and Others, Conferred with the Hebrew* (London: John Day, 1562). See also: Beveridge, William, *A Defence of the Book of Psalms, collected into English metre, by Thomas Sternhold, John Hopkins, and Others. With critical observations on the late New Version [by N. Tate and N. Brady] compar'd with the Old* (London, 1710).

46

The White Gates,
Dorking, SURREY.

9th November, 1949.

Dear Mueller Hartman

I am so glad you can come on the 20th.

Do read the "Scholar Gipsy" and "Thyrsis"
which comes next to it in the book.

As regards the 104th Psalm you need not read
that except for the pleasure of reading such
magnificent language. My "Fantasia" is on the
tune of the metrical version of the 104th Psalm
in Sternhold & Hopkins and I only used one or two
verses for the sake of giving the choir something
to sing.

(R. Vaughan Williams).

R. Mueller-Hartmann, Esq.,
c/o J. Hornstein, Esq.,
Craigelly,
Ladyegate Road, Dorking.

No. 47
To Robert Müller-Hartmann[62]

The White Gates,
Dorking, SURREY.

23rd November, 1949.

Dear Müller-Hartmann

Thank you so much for your letter and its comments, which were just what I wanted.

I shall probably use the organ to play with the voices right at the end of the "Fantasia" so I hope the organists will be satisfied.[63]

Yrs

RVW

R. Mueller-Hartmann, Esq.,
Craigelly,
Ladyegate Road,
Dorking.

---

[62] Written as a reply to Müller-Hartmann's reaction to the "try through" performances at The White Gates on November 20, 1949.
[63] *Fantasia (Quasi Variazione) on the 'Old 104th' Psalm Tune.* An organist himself in early years, Vaughan Williams frequently uses humor when mentioning them.

47

The White Gates,
Dorking, SURREY.

23rd November, 1949.

Dear Mille-Hartman

Thank you so much for your letter and
its comments, which were just what I wanted.

I shall probably use the organ to play
with the voices right at the end of the "Fantasia"
so I hope the organist, will be satisfied.

yr aw

(R. Vaughan Williams).

R. Mueller-Hartmann, Esq.,
Craigelly,
Ladyegate Road,
Dorking.

No. 48
Note to Robert Müller-Hartmann

[1949-1950]

Music Examples: words from John Bunyan's *The Pilgrim's Progress* (with German Text) for preliminary discussions about the German translation of RVW's *The Pilgrim's Progress*[64]

Example 1
Pilger: "Was soll ich tun, daß ich selig werde?" (Pilgrim: "What shall I do to be saved?")
[Later used by RVW in Act I, Scene 1: The Pilgrim meets the Evangelist]

Example 2
Bote: ".. der Pilger." (Messenger: "[Hail], Pilgrim.")
[Later used by RVW in Act IV, Scene 2: The Shepherds of the Delectable Mountains]

Example 3
Wanton: "Und bei mir gibt's Singen und Tanzen." (Wanton: "I will give you singing and dancing.")
[Later used by RVW in Act III, Scene 1: Vanity Fair]

Example 4
Pilger: "..bist Du da." (Pilgrim: "..Thou art there.")
[Later used by RVW in Act III, Scene 2: The Pilgrim in Prison]

---

[64] See opera vocal score *The Pilgrim's Progress, A Morality in a Prologue, four Acts and an Epilogue, founded on John Bunyan's Allegory of the same name*, Libretto adapted by R. Vaughan Williams, with interpolations from the Bible and verse by Ursula Wood, German adaptation by Robert Müller-Hartmann and additions by Genia Hornstein (Oxford University Press, 1952).

48

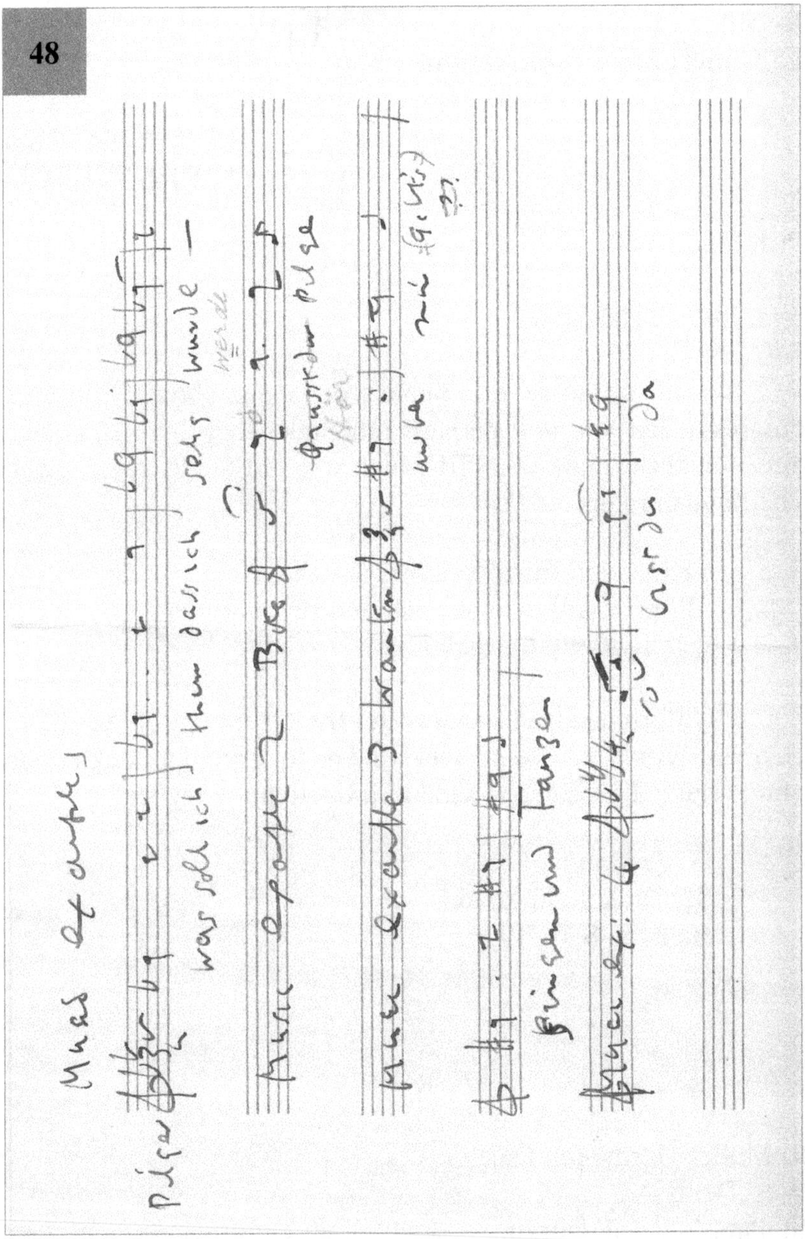

No. 49
To Robert Müller-Hartmann

The White Gates,
Dorking, SURREY.

11th May, 1950.

Dear Müller-Hartmann

I am so sorry to trouble you again about "Pilgrim's Progress", but you will perhaps remember that there is a stage direction at the end of Act III which was left out by my copyist. The English runs:

"The moon shines brighter and the
Pilgrim's Way is seen stretched
straight into the distance."

Unfortunately, I cannot find the typescript of Act III in German. Would you be so very kind as to write out the German of that stage direction and send it direct to my copyist:

G. de Mauny, Esq.,
82, Drakefield Road,
Balham, S.W. 17

Yrs

RVW

R. Müller-Hartmann, Esq.
West Dene,
St. Pauls's Road, Dorking.

49

The White Gates,
Dorking, SURREY.

11th May, 1950.

Müller - Hartmann

Dear ~~Müller~~

I am so sorry to trouble you again about
Pilgrim's Progress, but you will perhaps remember
that there is a stage direction at the end of
Act III which was left out by my copyist.   The
English runs:

"The moon shines brighter and the
Pilgrim's Way is seen stretched
straight into the distance."

Unfortunately I cannot find the typescript
of Act III in German.   Would you be so very kind
as to write out the German of that stage direction
and send it direct to my copyist:

G. de Mauny, Esq.,
82, Drakefield Road,
Balham,   S.W.17

(R. Vaughan Williams).

R. Müller-Hartmann, Esq.
West Dene,
St. Paul's Road,   Dorking.

No. 50
To Robert Müller-Hartmann

From R. Vaughan Williams,
The White Gates,
Westcott Road,
Dorking.

[1950]

Further to my letter of yesterday – there were two points which I forgot.

(i) <u>By-ends</u> "Stricter sort" – This does not mean orthodox in <u>doctrine</u> but strict in <u>conduct</u> – the "Orthodox" in Bunyan's time would be Church of England. Not very loose living – Probably By-ends himself was extremely orthodox as regards <u>Doctrine</u>.[65]

(ii) Act IV Bunyan Wallet = Reise Sack – I imagine the wallet was a small bag which hung on his belt – does not "Reise Sack" mean a port-manteau!(?)

RVW

---

[65] From Bunyan's *The Pilgrim's Progress*: By-ends: "'Tis true, we somewhat differ in religion from those of the stricter sort..."; Mr. Holy-man: "..and if their lives be loose, they will make the very name of a pilgrim stink."; and several references to Mr. Live-loose.

FROM R. VAUGHAN WILLIAMS,
THE WHITE GATES,
WESTCOTT ROAD,
DORKING.

TELEPHONE
DORKING 3055.

Further to my letter of
yesterday – there were

two points which I forgot

(1) By "ews" "Stricter
sort – This does not
mean orthodox in doctrine
but strict in conduct
– the "Orthodox" in Bunyan's
time would be chapel
& English but very loose?

Byzantine

Pivy — Probably Byzantine
itself was entirely
orthodox as regards doctrine

Act IV Bunyan
(ii) Waller = Reise sack

— I imagine the waller
was a small bag which
hung on the belt ~~belt~~ belt   X
— Does not "Reise sack"
mean a portmanteau!??
            JW

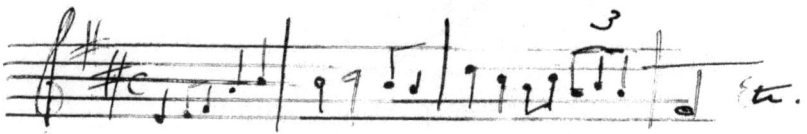

No. 51
To Robert Müller-Hartmann

The White Gates,
Dorking, SURREY.

24th May, 1950.

Dear Müller-Hartmann

Would you mind advising me what I ought to do about
the enclosed?

Does the word "meinung" mean "opinion" and do they
really suggest that I should give an opinion on Bach?!!

Yrs

R. Vaughan Williams

R. Müller-Hartmann, Esq.,
West Dene,
St. Paul's Road,
Dorking.

Encl.

51

The White Gates,
Dorking,   SU.REY.

24th May, 1950.

Dea Muller-Hertman

    Would you mind advising me what I ought
to do about the enclosed?

    Does the word "meinung" mean "opinion"
and do they really suggest that I should give
an opinion on Bach? !!

                 s a Vaughan

           (R. Vaughan Williams).

R. Müller-Hartmann, Esq.,
West Dene,
St. Paul's Road,
Dorking.

Encl.

No. 52
To Robert Müller-Hartmann

The White Gates,
Dorking, SURREY.

9th August, 1950.

Dear Müller-Hartmann

Thank you so much for that interesting quotation, which I entirely agree with. I once heard a performance broadcast from Leipzig, where they ought to know. It seemed to me one of the worst I ever heard.

Please thank Marianne[66] very much for so kindly translating it for me.

The Fourth Act of the Opera[67] is out, and I shall hope soon to be able to send you a copy.

Yrs

R. Vaughan Williams

R. Müller-Hartmann, Esq.
West Dene,
St. Paul's Rd., Dorking.

---

[66] The Hornstein's oldest daughter.
[67] *The Pilgrim's Progress*.

52

The White Gates,
Dorking, SURREY.

9th August, 1950.

Dear Miller Hartman

      Thank you so much for that interesting
quotation, which I entirely agree with.   I once
heard a performance broadcast from Leipzig, where
they ought to know.   It seemed to me one of the
worst I had ever heard.

      Please thank Marianne very much for so
kindly translating it for me.

      The Fourth Act of the Opera is out, and
I shall hope soon to be able to send you a copy.

          R Vaughan

(R. Vaughan Williams).

R. Miller-Hartmann, Esq.
West Dene,
St. Paul's Rd., Dorking.

No. 53
To Mrs. Müller-Hartmann

The White Gates
Dorking

Oct 17 [year not determined]

Dear Mrs Müller-Hartmann

Thank you both so much for your part of my lovely present.[68] It was a great pleasure to see you at the studio on Monday.

Yrs

R. Vaughan Williams

---

[68] Vaughan Williams's birth date is October 12, 1872.

53

The White Gates
Dorking
Oct 18

Dear Mrs Miller-Hutman

Thank you both so
much for your dear
& very lovely present.
It was a great
pleasure to see you
at the studio & thank you

R Vaughan Williams

No. 54
To the Müller-Hartmanns

The White Gates
Dorking

Oct 16 [year not determined]

My Dear Friends

Thank you both for your good wishes – I wish you could have been at the concert & the party.

By the way the Radio message transported your signatures into "Hornste[in] Susanne Müller and Hartmann"!![69]

Yrs

R. Vaughan Williams

---

[69] Probably celebrating Vaughan Williams's birthday, October 12th. Presumably the Hornsteins had signed on the same line.

54

The White Gates

Dorking

Oct 16

My Dear Friend

Thank you both for your

kind wishes — I wish you

both have been or to

Concert — the lady

By the way the Radio nestle

transposed your Signature into

" Horiste Susanng Muller
and Hartmann " !!

as

a sayhulan

No. 55
To Robert Müller-Hartmann[70]

The White Gates,
Dorking, SURREY.

8th September, 1950.

<u>Telephone</u>: Dorking 3055.

Dear Müller-Hartmann

    The Oxford Press are at last going to print the "Partita".[71] Would it be asking you too much to ask you to go through the manuscript score and see if there is anything in your opinion which wants altering before they print it?

    I feel you should do this, as the work belongs so much to you, and I should value your suggestions and corrections very much.

Yrs

R. Vaughan Williams

R. Müller-Hartmann, Esq.
West Dene,
St. Paul's Road,
Dorking.

---

[70] Possibly the last letter written to Müller-Hartmann before his death on December 15, 1950.
[71] *Partita for Double String Orchestra*, on which Müller-Hartmann assisted.

176

55

The White Gates,
Dorking,   SURREY.

8th September, 1950.

Telephone:Dorking 3065.

Dr Miller Hartmann

      The Oxford Press are at last going to
print the "Partita".   Would it be asking you too
much to ask you to go through the manuscript
score and see if there is anything in your opinion
which wants altering before they print it?

      I feel you should do this, as the work
belongs so much to you, and I should value your
suggestions and corrections very much.

(R. Vaughan Williams).

R. Müller-Hartmann, Esq.
West Dene,
St. Paul's Road,
Dorking.

No. 56
To Mrs. Müller-Hartmann[72]

May 12, 1951 [per postmark]

Mrs Müller-Hartmann
West Dene
St. Paul's Road
Dorking

    Thank you very much for your kind sympathy.

              R. Vaughan Williams

---

[72] Acknowledging the death of Adeline Vaughan Williams who died on May 10, 1951.

56

POST CARD

DORKING
5 30 PM
12 MAY
1951
SURREY

POSTAGE

Mrs Miller-Hartmann
Westdene
St Pauls Road
Dorking

Thankyou very much for your
Kind sympathy
R Vaughan Williams

No. 57
To Mrs. Müller-Hartmann

The White Gates,
Dorking, Surrey.

24th November, 1951.

Telephone: Dorking 3055.

Dear Mrs. Müller-Hartmann,

I have now received from the printers Mr. Müller-Hartmann's original copy of my "Partita".[73]

I thought perhaps you would like to have it so I am sending it by registered post.

Yours sincerely,

R. Vaughan Williams

Mrs. Müller-Hartmann,
West Dene,
St. Paul's Rd.,
Dorking.

---

[73] *Partita for Double String Orchestra.* Susanne Müller-Hartmann donated the score to the British Library in 1980.

The White Gates,
              Dorking, Surrey.
                24th November, 1951.
Telephone: Dorking 3055.

Dear Mrs. Müller-Hartmann,

        I have now received from the
printers Mr. Müller-Hartmann's original
copy of my "Partita".

        I thought perhaps you would like
to have it so I am sending it by
registered post.

                Yours sincerely,

                R Vaughan Williams

                (R. Vaughan Williams).

Mrs. Müller-Hartmann,
West Dene,
St. Paul's Rd.,
Dorking.

No. 58
To Mrs. Müller-Hartmann

From R. Vaughan Williams,
The White Gates,
Westcott Road,
Dorking.

September 18, 1952 [per postmark]

With kind regards.

From

R. Vaughan Williams

Mrs Miller Hartmann

West Dene

St Pauls Road

Dorking

Surrey

FROM R. VAUGHAN WILLIAMS,

THE WHITE GATES,

WESTCOTT ROAD,

DORKING.

TELEPHONE
DORKING 3055.

With kid regards

L

R Vaughanwilliams

No. 59
To Mrs. Müller-Hartmann

From R. Vaughan Williams,
The White Gates,
Westcott Road,
Dorking.

October 14th 1952.

Dear Mrs Müller-Hartmann,

How did you guess I liked Earl Grey? Thank you so much for remembering my birthday.[74]

Give my love to Susan and thank her for her share in the present.

Yours sincerely,

R. Vaughan Williams

---

[74] October 12, 1872. Robert Müller-Hartmann died in 1950; Lisbeth and Susanne Müller-Hartmann were still living at West Dene.

Mrs Muller Hartmann,

West Dean,

St Paul's road,

Dorking.

FROM R. VAUGHAN WILLIAMS,

THE WHITE GATES,

WESTCOTT ROAD,

DORKING.

TELEPHONE
DORKING 3055

October 14th 1952.

Dear Mrs Muller Hartmann,

How did you guess I
liked Earl Grey ? Thank you xxdx so
much for remembering my birthday.

Give my love to Susan
and thank her for her share in the
present.

Yours sincerely,

R Vaughan Williams

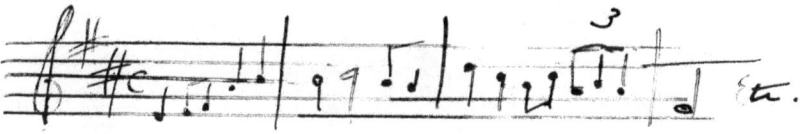

No. 60
To Mrs. Müller-Hartmann from Ursula and Ralph
Vaughan Williams

[1953-1957]

With affectionate X-mas greetings

From

Ursula
and Ralph
Vaughan Williams[75]

---

[75] Ursula Wood and Ralph Vaughan Williams were married on February 7, 1953.

With affectionate Xmas
greetings

for

Ursula.

and Ralph

r aybnd changes

Bibliography

Bunyan, John, *The Pilgrim's Progress* (1678).

Cobbe, Hugh, *Letters of Ralph Vaughan Williams* (Oxford University Press, 2008).

The Emergency Committee in Aid of Displaced Foreign Scholars Records (1927-1949), Manuscripts and Archives Division, The New York Public Library.

Kennedy, Michael, *A Catalogue of the Works of Ralph Vaughan Williams*, 2nd edn. (Oxford University Press, 1996).
    The Oxford Dictionary of Music (Oxford University Press, 1985).
    The Works of Ralph Vaughan Williams (Oxford University Press, 1964).

Manx National Heritage Library, *Internment During World Wars I & II* (Isle of Man Government, 2006).

Vaughan Williams, Ursula, *Paradise Remembered: An Autobiography* (Albion Music Ltd., 2002).
    R.V.W.: A Biography of Ralph Vaughan Williams (Oxford University Press, 1964).

Zenck, Claudia Maurer, Peter Petersen and Sophie Fetthauer, *Lexicon verfolgter Musiker und Musikerinnen der NS-Zeit (LexM)* [Encyclopedia of Persecuted Musicians of the NS-Time] (University of Hamburg, 2005).

Index

www.ingramcontent.com/pod-product-compliance
Lightning Source LLC
Chambersburg PA
CBHW030937150426
42812CB00064B/2982/J